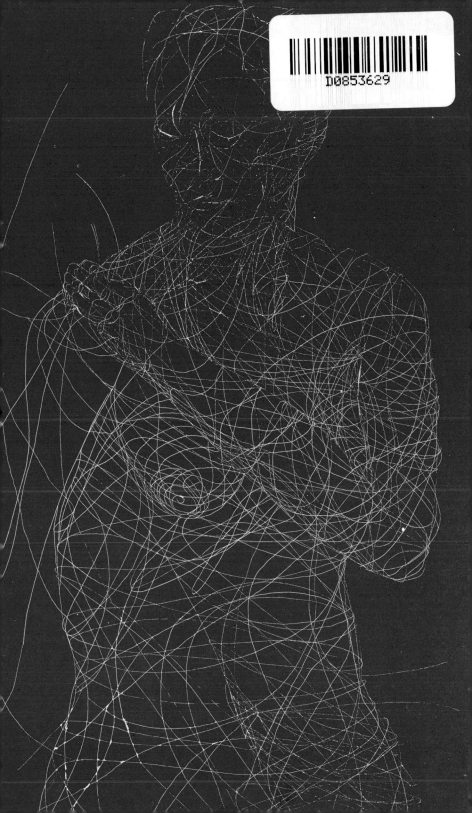

Communication
Philosophy
and the
Technological
Age

Edited by
Michael J. Hyde

The University of Alabama Press
University, Alabama

Library of Congress Cataloging in Publication Data

Main entry under title:

Communication philosophy and the technological
   age.

   Revised versions of 5 lectures given at a
symposium held at the University of Alabama in
the spring of 1980.
   Bibliography: p.
   Includes index.
   1. Communication—Philosophy—Congresses.
2. Technological innovations—Congresses.
I. Hyde, Michael J., 1950–
P96.T42C6   001.51'01   81–3420
ISBN 0–8173–0077–5   AACR2

DEDICATION

To my parents,
Howard and Claire,
with much love and admiration

Contents

Preface

In the spring semester of 1980, the College of Arts and Sciences at The University of Alabama sponsored a symposium entitled "Communication Philosophy: The Human Condition in a Technological Age." Supported by a grant from the University, the symposium sought to explore the question: What effects does the intensification of technology have upon the structure and dynamics of human communication? Five distinguished scholars were invited to present public lectures directed toward a philosophical examination of the question and to participate in the symposium meetings during their separate visits. These scholars were Edward G. Ballard, Don Ihde, Henry W. Johnstone, Jr., John O'Neill, and Calvin O. Schrag.

The five essays comprising this collection are revised versions of the public lectures. These essays are arranged here not in the order of their presentation as public lectures but according to relationships that may be seen if the essays are read serially. An introductory essay has been added to facilitate an appreciation of how the essays relate to an important perspective within the current debate concerning technology. This perspective, as explained in the introduction, is termed "communication philosophy."

Clearly, research in communication philosophy is not a new enterprise; a basic understanding of Greek and Roman philosophy brings an awareness that our learned ancestors were much concerned with how communicative behavior relates to the human condition. Within the field of communication today, scholars continue to encourage and advance this concern; for with the acceleration of technological change during the twentieth century, human communicative behavior has undergone a transformation that requires a philosophical comprehension beyond that set forth by our ancestors. Put simply, human communicative behavior in today's technological society encompasses more than "the good man speaking well." By addressing the question posed as the topic of these essays from the perspective of communication philosophy, the five scholars not only suggest what this transformation entails but provide important directives for gauging some of the consequences that may arise as technological change accelerates in the future.

This collection of essays owes much not only to its contributors but also to many individuals who were generous with their time, their intellect, and their enthusiasm. At the risk of omitting someone whom my memory has lost, I wish to express gratitude to the following people: Professors Jan Nelson, Daniel Pound, Charles Self, E. Culpepper Clark, George H. Wolfe, Douglas E. Jones, and Richard A. Krause, for their continued support of the project and for their invaluable insights concerning technology and human communication; Malcolm MacDonald, director of The University of Alabama Press, and his staff, for their expert assistance in bringing this collection to fruition; Trudie Calvert, for being a talented and devoted copyeditor; Gayle Griffin and Kevin Peterson, for being superior graduate student assistants; Charles Mandly, Jr., and Katherine Alexander, for their scholarly presence; Gloria Keller and Peggy Caffee, for their cherished secretarial abilities; the student members of the symposium, for their ever challenging minds; and my wife, Bobette, for her love.

Introduction: The Debate Concerning Technology

Michael J. Hyde

Many scholars argue that technology is the sine qua non of most genuinely great human achievements. Others reply, with equal vigor, that technology is leading to the dehumanization of man. This debate between the advocates and the critics of technology, wherein technology's human component is both exalted and pitied, has produced contradictory expectations concerning the future of humankind.

Advocates of technology maintain that the human component is best defined and advanced in terms of technological progress, because such progress is guided by scientific criteria. Under this guidance the development of techniques is given priority so that these techniques can aid in the explanation, prediction, and control of the ambiguous human condition. Technical understanding *first*, human understanding *second*, become the procedural steps of technological progress. The priority is clear for those adhering to the spirit of such progress: "Our clearest and most fruitful knowledge is not knowledge of ourselves or of how we communicate. Rather it is knowledge of various physical and chemical processes. That knowledge has enabled us to make powerful tools that have changed our lives greatly. We understand these tools far better than we understand ourselves."[1]

Critics of technology, on the other hand, see their adversaries' position as fostering a technological conscience that is allowing technology to become out-of-control and deterministic.[2] These critics question the supposed dependency of the human component on technology; they suggest that the autonomy of the human component must be realized. Such a realization, argue these critics, cannot be achieved through a passive allegiance to the priority of technological progress. Guided only by this priority, the essence of "human" being becomes both alienated and misunderstood.

Like most debates, the debate concerning technology, at first glance, suggests an either/or situation: either one is for technology or one is against it; technology, love it or leave it. This conception of the debate, however, is too simple; it is based on and fosters a knee-jerk mentality that, when allowed to structure the debate, inhibits the communicative capacity of the interlocutors and thus precludes a tenable solution to the controversy. Nevertheless, the conception and its founding mentality are operative today and contribute to the division between what C. P. Snow in 1959 called "the two cultures" of academic life—those adhering to a "scientific-technological" world-view versus those identifying themselves as "humanists." While this division may allow the respective camps to meet the demands of specialization required by the bureaucratic organization of the university, it also has made the impossibility of communication a growing possibility. That is, as specialization requires scholars to engulf themselves in the cryptic languages of technology, mathematics, philosophy, literary history, and so on, these scholars develop a trained incapacity to translate and communicate their acquired knowledge to others. This "problem of communication," according to Bruce Watkins and Roy Meador, "is aggravated by the fact that the demands of specialization often leave no energy or interest for the intellectual fertilization derived from exploring other fields and cultures."[3] The schism grows as it becomes easier to abide by a bifurcated vision of the world that subjects itself to the principle of the "excluded middle."

This either/or situation is by no means confined to the university. When the specialists are forced to address and resolve exigencies spawned by technological occurrences in the everyday world, these specialists must include the general public in their debate. This amorphous "mass" of nonspecialists—who are obliged to wait for deciphered versions of sophisticated knowledge to filter down into the zeitgeist, who use this knowledge to identify the various halls of academe by reading and "knowing" the inscriptions (e.g., $E = Mc^2$, "Know Thy Self") written above portals, who so often do not know that they do not know[4]—requires and demands guidance when confronting the anomalies of technology.

Acquiescing to this demand is no easy task for the specialist. A rhetoric must be found that both pacifies the trepidations of the mass and accurately reflects the point of view of the rhetor/specialist. Realizing, however, that public visibility can be a genuine liability to academic respectability, the specialist is oftentimes compelled not to reveal in great detail wherefrom he or she speaks.[5] Hence, guided by this notion of academic elitism—"The mass crushes beneath it everything that is different, everything that is excellent, individual, qualified and select"[6]—the option to answer the public's demand in simplistic terms of either/or becomes inviting and perhaps necessary. Consider, for example, the "bottom-line" rhetoric offered to and appropriated by the public to explain the recent breakdown of the nuclear reactor at Three Mile Island. Advocates of technology labeled the situation an "accident" attributable to "human error"; critics of technology conceived it as a "disaster" warranting the antitechnological conclusion "no more nukes!"

Armed with this rhetoric of either/or, the general public is free to join the debate concerning technology. And as the simplicity of such rhetoric reifies both the thinking and the behavior of the public, the public's response to technology approaches what Dostoevsky, in his *Notes from Underground*, described as the antithesis between the "normal man" (those people who unquestioningly accept and are morally soothed by the scientific basis of technological progress) and the "hyperconscious man" (those people who speak out against their technological subservience).[7] William Barrett's description of the public behavior that approximates such an antithesis suggests the danger of understanding technology from an either/or perspective:

> We rail at technology when it gets too noisy, pollutes our air, or is about to drive a new superhighway through our living room. For the rest, we are content to consume its products unquestioningly. So long as we can negotiate the triumph of technology successfully, we are unconcerned to ask what the presuppositions of this technical world are and how they bind us to its framework. Already these presuppositions are so much the invisible medium of our actual world that we have become unconscious of them.[8]

We trust technology when it works; we distrust and want to abandon technology when it makes us feel uncomfortable. Throughout our lives we tend to be either the "normal man" or the "hyperconscious man." As the "normal man" we grow content with that which we do not question, technology. As the "hyperconscious man" we scorn that which we have come not to understand, technology. Hence, the danger is not technology; rather, the danger is us—we who do not question, we who do not understand, we who do not communicate beyond the rhetoric of either/or.

To eliminate this danger requires that technology be scrutinized with a philosophical rigor that moves beyond the limitations of either/or, where questioning elucidates understanding, where understanding promotes open communication, and where such communication, whenever necessary, encourages additional questioning. This dialectical progression of questioning-understanding-communication is the hallmark of philosophical inquiry. Here the rhetoric of either/or is for-

bidden, for such rhetoric impedes communication and thus
the "aim" and "demand" of philosophy. Karl Jaspers makes
this same point:

> Communication . . . is the aim of philosophy, and in com-
> munication all its other aims are ultimately rooted. . . .
> What is not realized in communication is not yet, what is
> not ultimately grounded in it is without adequate foundation.
> The truth begins with two.
> Consequently philosophy demands: seek constant com-
> munication, risk it without reserve, renounce the defiant self-
> assertion which forces itself upon you in ever new disguises,
> live in the hope that in your very renunciation you will in
> some incalculable way be given back to yourself.[9]

To maintain, as Jaspers does, that communication requires
a renunciation of self-assertion is to acknowledge the dialectical relationship that communication enters into with questioning and understanding when communication is performed
openly. The dynamics of this relationship can be illustrated by
observing how the relationship should be promoted within
the debate concerning technology.

Open communication begins with questioning, or more
specifically, with reflection. "Reflection is the courage to
question as deeply as possible the truth of our own presuppositions and the exact place of our own aims,"[10] as such aims
are directed toward an understanding of specific objects of
inquiry (e.g., technology). Reflection, and not merely "the
stating of one's glands," must become the critical impulse
when investigating technology. Without such reflection the
questioning of technology oftentimes becomes nothing more
than the zealous attempts of advocates and critics of technology to advance their particular interests (e.g., religious, political, economic). Interests, however, are biases, favored ways
of approaching and understanding one's world for the purposes of acquiring knowledge. And although one's interests

can evolve from a personal commitment to one's disciplinary training—as such training enhances the belief that herein lies the road to truth—interests too often encourage one to observe and understand a phenomenon only in terms of what one already has in mind.[11] Here, an understanding of technology becomes distorted, for what is understood is not technology and its presuppositions but technology clothed in the presuppositions of a particular interest. Any assertion about technology, when communicated on the basis of such understanding, is more an expression of self than it is of technology. Self-assertion flourishes when left unchecked by critical reflection. Within this flourishing of self-assertion lie the rhetorical roots of either/or, because, as with the Three Mile Island situation mentioned earlier, conflicting self-assertions uninspired by critical reflection often lead to communication marked only by contradiction.

Critical reflection, however, serves to "bracket" the presuppositions of both an interest and its accompanying self-assertion. In so doing, it allows the "thing itself" under investigation (e.g., technology and its presuppositions) to assume the guiding role for acquiring understanding. One must come to understand technology; technology must not be made to assume the form of either this interest or that interest. If technology and its presuppositions have become "the invisible medium of our actual world" (Barrett), and if this medium is to be taken notice of and understood in an accurate way, then this medium must be allowed to speak in its own voice. Only then can one's communication about technology be open to that of which one speaks. Responses to this communication must, in turn, echo the teachings of technology and not merely the teachings underlying one's interests. Whether the teachings of technology are today beneficial and/or detrimental must be determined within this open arena of communication. The debate concerning technology must therefore become a debate given over to conversation, a dialectical progression of questioning-understanding-communication, wherein both advocates and critics of technology allow themselves "to be conducted by the object to which the parties in the conversation are directed."[12] An example of how this dialectical progression can move one toward a rigorous assessment of technology is found in the literature dealing with technology's relationship to science and this relationship's effects on both nature and human behavior.

The history of modern technology is, at the same time, a history of science. That is, the growth of modern technology is in great part the result of technology's appropriation of such scientific values as "measurement" and "rationality" for the purposes of "problem solving," "cognitive control," and "work."[13] This appropriation of science by technology sparked much debate between scholars concerned with identifying and distinguishing technology from the enterprise of science. One common but fundamental distinction that arose in the debate is suggested by I. C. Jarvie, who notes that, unlike the overriding aim of science, "truth is not the overriding aim of technology. . . . If the aim is to manage to accomplish something practical which science allows as not impossible, rather than to discover some universal truth, then technology is what we call it."[14] With this philosophical appreciation of technology emerged the general conclusion that technology serves only an instrumental function—it is a prescribed means to a desired end. Science, on the other hand, serves to instruct the instrumentality of technology through "calculative" reasoning. That is, science enhances technology's ability to order its instrumentality in such a way that a desired, preprogrammed outcome is calculable in advance.

Such reflections on the relationship between technology and science not only enhanced an understanding of each enterprise but also established a common ground from which scholars could communicate about how technology, under the guidance of science, affects both nature and human behavior.

For instance, a crucial point made by scholars was this: What nature is ordered to be under the means-end function of technology's calculative instrumentality reveals itself in terms of the selected means that accomplish the ordering. When the objects of nature are transformed in this way, the objects are reduced to a function that directly corresponds with the ordering means. The object's standing *qua* object is thereby reserved to promote only the "telic inclination" of the means.[15] A researcher who, for example, uses an "instrument" to measure a person's communicative apprehension is a case in point, for here, as in any scientific-technological procedure, the researcher's primary responsibility must be to the "correct" use of the instrument, not to the person's general problem. The problem is thereby reduced so that it can conform to and thus reproduce the desired technical effect of the instrument.[16]

That technology's instrumentality has such an effect on nature and that this effect, in turn, demands a sense of responsibility on the part of a human being for maintaining this instrumentality led scholars to identify the control factor inherent in "technological operations" (or what is often referred to as "techniques"). This control factor can be stated as follows: Behavior that is not conducive to a given technique's instrumentality tends to be reduced or eliminated by the technique. Consider, for example, the behavior of reflective thinking as it can be used when composing a discourse at a typewriter, as compared to composing with a pen or a pencil. For most people the typewriter, unlike the pen or the pencil, will restrict reflective thinking because to think about what you are typing, as you are typing it, often results in mistakes. (Professional typists are trained not to think about the manuscripts they are typing for this very reason.) More specifically, the typewriter's mode of operation, unlike the pen's or the pencil's, is designed primarily for speed, not for contemplation; it thus inclines the user to a certain style of behavior that is conducive to its "normative and functionally optimal use." As Don Ihde points out, "The telic inclination made possible by the instrument [e.g., the typewriter] does not cut off any human aim through itself, although it does call for varying degrees of effort on the part of the user to counter whatever may be the implicit rhythm of the instrument in its normative and functionally optimal use."[17] When such effort remains passive to the instrument's telic inclination, the "proper" technique of typing controls the user's behavior. Hence, reflective thinking diminishes; technique proliferates.

Admittedly, the above discussion of technology's relationship to science and this relationship's effects on both nature and human behavior provides but a brief illustration of what the literature has to offer concerning these topics. The discussion, however, was not intended to be comprehensive; rather, its purpose was to show how a philosophical appreciation of technology has been acquired, an appreciation founded on a dialectical progression of questioning, understanding, and communication. To the extent that this mode of inquiry continues to mark the path for those engaged in the debate concerning technology, the debate can perhaps avoid the rhetorical pitfalls of either/or.

The present collection of essays is an attempt to promote this mode of inquiry as it can instruct a contemporary assessment of technology's effects on the human condition. Specifically, the five essays offer a philosophical reply to the question: What effects does the intensification of technology have upon the structure and dynamics of human communication?[18] That human communication plays a major role in ordering the ambiguity of the human condition suggests the importance of this question. In addressing the question philosophically, the authors make communication not only a goal but also an object of investigation. The communication philosophy that emerges in and through the essays is the result of each author's reflection on the presuppositions of certain aspects of technology, as these aspects and their presuppositions take form and thereby show themselves in human communicative behavior. How such technologically inspired behavior differs from or is similar to the goal of open communication (which the authors hope to accomplish by performing this initial step for acquiring a philosophical appreciation of the question) should suggest something about the beneficial and/or detrimental effects of technology on human communication in particular and on the human condition in general.

Edward Ballard begins the inquiry with an examination of dialectical processes. Ballard conceives dialectic as "a communicative process by which experience grows," a process crucial to mechanical-technological and biological systems, as well as to human involvements. By examining the "different kinds or species" of dialectic as they present themselves in various contexts, Ballard shows that dialectic does not retain "the same specific [communicative] sense when referred to mechanical and biological systems . . . as it possesses when referred to human involvements." The differences elucidated here enable Ballard to suggest what happens when the dialectic of human involvements takes on the characteristics of the dialectic underlying mechanical routines. In this transformation develops what Ballard labels the "technological dialectic of man and machine," a dialectic that he believes may not be favorable to humankind and its creative growth.

Henry Johnstone's discussion of technology and human communication provides an important extension of Ballard's essay in that Johnstone's discussion develops around the concept of "creativity." Johnstone contends that a major threat posed by technology today is its restriction of authentic dialogue—the creative form of human communication. Johnstone dramatizes this threat by showing what creativity entails, how creativity is not characteristic of technological processes, how dialogue fosters creative communication, how such communication can be formulated into an ethics, and how communication violates this ethics when communication becomes technological.

Don Ihde's reflections on technology and human communication complement both Ballard's and Johnstone's observations, for Ihde performs a phenomenology "of common media-embodied communication situations to point up and isolate the specifically invariant features of the technological transformation of human communication." Ihde argues that the transformation of "face-to-face" dialogical situations by technologies introduces a "third factor" into these situations such that the situations become "mediated." In our advanced technological society, according to Ihde, we tend to take for granted this commonplace occurrence; hence, we fail to comprehend a variety of effects that technology imposes on the communicative dimension of the human condition. By uncovering some presuppositions of these effects, Ihde elucidates manipulative features of technology that both restrict and facilitate human communicative behavior.

John O'Neill's contribution helps to illustrate how some of the observations offered in the preceding three essays can direct cultural analyses of technology and its effects on human communication. O'Neill offers an interpretive reading of the "American Way of Life," as this life and its communicative impulse have become dominated by a technological process directed toward the materialization and the commercialization of ideals expressed in the Declaration of Independence. To demonstrate the effects of this process and its underlying mentality, O'Neill interprets various "artifacts" of communicative media (e.g., a restaurant's place mat, commercials, urban graffiti) that epitomize the "revelation" of technology in American life and, at the same time, "subvert the deepest, the most trivial, the most holy, and the most vulgar of our beliefs and values."

Calvin Schrag's essay provides a fitting conclusion to this collection. By examining the communicative role played by the university in a technological age, Schrag focuses on the environment in which the debate concerning technology receives much of its direction. The responsibility the university owes to the debate is made clear by Schrag: "It may well be that the most demanding challenge of the modern-day university is to coexist with technology without becoming technologized." According to Schrag, when a university becomes "technologized," its essential status as a "community" is transformed into a managerial technocracy. By suggesting what such a transformation entails and how it affects communication, Schrag enables us to see the university as a paradigm for gauging many of the observations contained in this collection.

To appreciate the communication philosophy offered by each of these authors as they reflect on today's technological society requires that one enter into the dialogue not as an advocate or as a critic of technology but simply as an open-minded person. This requirement must be taken seriously if the reflections contemplated here are to promote understanding and communication. For the skeptic who sees this "aim" and "demand" of philosophy to be nothing but an exercise in speculative knowledge and thereby devoid of any value, I can relate but one more directive offered by Gabriel Marcel when he spoke of philosophy's role in technological developments:

> [A] civilization in which technical progress is tending to emancipate itself more and more from speculative knowledge, and finally to question the traditional rights of speculative knowledge, a civilization which, one may say, finally denies the place of contemplation and shuts out the very possibility of contemplation, such a civilization, I say, sets us inevitably on the road towards a philosophy which is not so much a *love of wisdom* as a *hatred of wisdom*: we ought rather to call it a misosophy. [19]

The road *not* taken by the following essays is that of "misosophy."

On Dialectic:
Mechanical and Human

Edward Goodwin Ballard

I will consider here a pattern of action, thought, and communication called dialectic, a pattern ubiquitous if not universal, one in which all of us are often caught up. And because we are caught in it, doubtless it is better for us to be aware of its nature and possible turnings than to submit to it ignorantly and passively. This important communicative pattern of thought and action suffers from having had more said about it than has been understood.

Dialectic is a process directed in part by its own outcome. It might be said to be in a certain sense a self-corrective pattern of discovery and renewal. But we need to move more deliberately toward an understanding of these statements about dialectic through an analysis of different kinds or species and through illustrations of the process.

Dialectic names a communicative process by which experience grows. We are always in the midst of this process. We are aware of the interaction of feelings, images, recollections, and concepts functioning as principles of interpretation and directed upon presented objects, events, other persons, and the like. By "principle of interpretation" I mean any concept, image, rule, habit, and the like, which we may use to give any meaning whatsoever to that which is experienced. By this process, things become familiar, and familiar things are overlaid with other values, imaginings, beliefs, and knowledge, for once presentations have received some interpretation, some identification, they may be given all sorts of additional meanings.

Is there a recognizable initial stage of this process of interpretation? Perhaps we may assume that pure or completely
uninterpreted presentations are initially interpreted by basic
categories. In fact, I see no alternative to this assumption. But
that we are not ordinarily aware of any such initial stage of
interpretation, bringing together two pristine and isolated
factors, seems evident and verifiable. Even hypothetical re-
constructions of early infantile experience indicate no such
initial stage. At every phase of actual awareness, our flow of
feeling, presentations, imagery, and memory exhibit some
organization, some testimony to prior interpretation. It is as if
the dialectical process had always already begun. Formal or
empty categories and pure (uninterpreted) presentations,
then, may come to be related through dialectic, but in every
instance of experience they have already been so related.

Although the initial phase of the dialectical process does not
fall within our purview, we can observe the progress of dialectic and perhaps grasp its structure. Thereupon, we may develop a general description of it, define it, take note of its
fundamental forms, offer some illustrations of it, and finally
discuss briefly some of the problems related to its direction of
movement and to its evaluation.

The Generic Sense of Dialectic

In fourth-century Greece dialectic referred to a well-
regulated conversation in which the participants, by the exchange of information and ideas, brought one another into a
state of agreement or at least mutual understanding. Many
philosophers have believed, though, that the pattern of such
an interchange is involved in very many contexts other than
the conversational. Some of these contexts are simpler than
the conversational. In them the exchange of information is
easier to follow and the relations are more easily distinguished. We shall begin with the simpler contexts and work

our way into the more complex, and in so doing we shall be able to abstract more than one form of the pattern of dialectic. Also, the scope and limitations of dialectic will need to be indicated. An acceptable and general first definition of this term may be found, I believe, if it is specified as a causal relation, holding between entities of a certain kind, and related to an end.

This causal relation is exemplified in many different kinds of occasions, for example, in efficient causation where contact with one particle is the sufficient condition for the change in momentum and velocity of another, and where the causing particle undergoes an alteration as a result of the impact. The momentum might be passed along an indefinitely long linear series of particles in this manner. This causal relation is exemplified in organic systems and in neuropsychological changes. Likewise, in a logical sense, premises are said to be the sufficient condition or cause of the conclusion, and certain theories of induction attempt to set up conditions under which the data might be said to cause the theory based upon them.

Some restriction is placed upon the generality of the definition of the causal relation by noting that the entities it can relate must be at least partly homogeneous. The momentum of a billiard ball does not somehow cause a thought to appear in another billiard ball; the effect must be analogous to the cause. The causal event can communicate only such characteristics as it already possesses. This communicated element may be thought of as a structure. The moving billiard ball is a mass-force structure. It alters the mass-force structure of the ball upon which it impinges so that the two are more nearly similar in structure, i.e., the former gives up some of its momentum to the latter. This kind of correspondence between cause and effect was phrased by the medievals as an axiom: like causes like. Bertrand Russell has given this axiom a modern turn in his generalization: "It appears generally that if A and B are two complex structures and A can cause B, then there must be some degree of identity of structure between A and B."[1] For present purposes, this expression of the partial structural identity between cause and effect is introduced to define the kind of entity that can enter into a causal relation. It limits the causal relation to holding among partially homogeneous entities. An occasion of causation is an occasion where some identity in structure is communicated from one event to another.

It will be useful to distinguish linear causal relations, as in the example of the billiard balls, from cyclical ones. To make this transition an intermediate notion is needed: reciprocal causality.

Suppose A and B are events in a relatively isolated system (A might be a ship's heading, B might be the rudder angle), then if A, perhaps through intermediaries, causes an effect in B, A will be changed as a consequence; such events are said to be related by reciprocal causality. But this statement is scarcely other than a generalized statement of Newton's third law. If, though, the relation between A and B is continuously reciprocal, the situation is altered. The change effected in B will react back on A, yielding A'. Then the A' will react in a somewhat different way upon the B, producing B', and so on. Thus a system of continuously and mutually changing events or entities is set up; this system may be called a cyclical system. When the relation of continuous reciprocal causality holds among events, then these events may be said to be related dialectically, using the term in a very general or generic sense, or to interact dialectically.

Consider a linear causal series, in which A causes B and B causes C, etc.; one can scarcely refer to an end of the series in any sense other than as a final temporal member of the series. In the cyclical or dialectical system, however, again the situation is different. For this kind of system moves in a direction; it moves in one specifiable manner rather than in another.

The notion of end is a convenient way of defining this direction. The notion of end, however, is moot; it will be discussed in the next section. Here it is sufficient to note that a dialectical system of mutually changing elements, A and B, changes in the direction of the accommodation of A to B, an accommodation or similarity that was expressed by reference to their sharing a common structure or pattern. The end as specified so far of the movement is the complete accommodation of A to B. Such a dialectical movement is often characterized as an evolution. It is illustrated by species of living beings that have, through the process usually described as mutation and natural selection, adapted themselves with increasing efficiency to the peculiarities of an environment.

Such a dialectical system will be continuously in the process of altering its characteristics while, in virtue of the principle of similarity of cause and effect, preserving some identity of structure. Dialectic is the changer changing in a continuous process.

We need to consider some illustrations of this continuous reciprocal causality. I choose a simple mechanical illustration that will indicate some further detail of this causal linkage— the case of a ship which is kept on course by an automatic pilot. The ship is, say, on a northerly course. Its heading changes to port (to the west), perhaps the result of waves beating on its starboard bow. An angle measuring device in the automatic pilot responds to this variation from the desired course, measures the angle of deviation, and sends electrical impulses proportional to this deviation to a machine that controls the rudder angle, turning the rudder to the right so as to compensate for the error in the ship's heading. The rudder then changes the ship's heading toward the desired course. The sensing device measures this smaller angle of error and communicates a new order to the output control and to the rudder, easing the rudder continuously until the ship is brought back on course. When the angle between the ship's heading and the desired course is zero, the rudder is amidships. Here the causal relation is made continuously reciprocal by (a) the "sensing device" that measures the angle of error, and (b) the "output control" that uses the latter measurement to control the ship's rudder. The end (telos, metaphorically understood) or state of mutual accommodation is reached when the ship's heading is identical with the desired course.

In old-fashioned steering machines the sensing device was a man, a pilot, whose eye and brain served to measure when and how far the ship was off course and whose hands (the output control) moved the tiller appropriately to compensate for this error and so to bring her back on course. These functions are all parts of the same person, the pilot, hence, they are not easily noticed separately. The mechanical device has the advantage of letting us see just how the effect, the ship's wandering off course, is communicated back to a cause, the steering engine, by way of (a) the device for sensing error, and (b) the device for output control. If, generally speaking, dialectic is the product controlling the production, then the dialectical relation always requires some such sensing or measuring device that evaluates the product at a given stage of the process and communicates this evaluation to an output control that determines the next step in the production.

A dialectical system, then, is exemplified on any occasion when distinguishable yet partly homogeneous events are related by some means to produce a causal arrangement that is continuously reciprocal and moves toward a state of mutual information. The means for producing a continuously reciprocal causal arrangement must fulfill at least two functions: (a) it must sense (measure) the deviation of the system from some preset state or state of equilibrium; (b) it must be capable of using this measurement to control the system and bring it closer to the preset state or state of equilibrium. Formally, then, dialectic is a relation of continuous, reciprocal causality that moves thus toward mutual accommodation or mutual information.

It should now be possible to distinguish, at least roughly, among dialectical systems by reference to the content, elements, or entities that enter into this dynamic relation. There may be a mechanical dialectic, like the automatic pilot, where the mutually changing elements are material bodies, or a biological dialectic in which the elements are organisms or families of organisms in the dynamic interrelationship with each other and with the environment. And surely there are various dialectical situations in which human beings participate. Later I shall consider three such situations: the (scientific) investigator and the data or objects he investigates; the person and his personal involvements; and the person and his modern technological environment. For the present, let us attend to the mechanical dialectic just illustrated by a ship's automatic pilot, because there is a question in the minds of many philosophers whether "dialectic" retains the same specific sense when referred to mechanical and biological systems (as we have been referring it) as it possesses when referred to human involvements. Let us consider these differences.

Generic and Specific Senses of Dialectic

The generic sense of dialectic developed in the preceding section should be clearly distinguished from the specific and, as it seems to me, more proper sense restricted in its reference to human contexts. The question devolves, of course, upon the interpretation of the meaning of the end toward which dialectic moves. True, efforts have been made within behavioristic and naturalistic contexts to naturalize such notions as purpose and movement toward an end. For example, in an important paper, "Behavior, Purpose, and Teleology," by Arturo Rosenblueth, Norbert Wiener, and Julian Bigelow,[2] the authors purport to effect just such a naturalization. This attempt was a failure; it is important to understand why it failed.

In accordance with their naturalistic categories, the authors of this paper define as "purposeful" any act that may be interpreted as behaving so as to reach "a definite correlation in time or in space with respect to another object or event" (p. 23). They offer as examples human voluntary activity and the behavior of some (not all) machines, specifically, those regulated by negative feedback so that they move toward a predesigned goal (and so are "teleological"). The reader will recognize in these machines allusion to the servomechanisms or self-regulating (cybernetic) machines with which Norbert Wiener's name has long been associated. A ship's automatic pilot offers a good illustration. The suggested implication is that human voluntary effort differs only in degree of complexity from the behavior of servomechanisms.

Despite the extraordinary success of these self-regulating machines and the degree to which they seem to imitate human intelligent activity, the appropriateness of using such terms as "purposeful" and "teleological" to describe their behavior is certainly to be questioned. Indeed, the question has been put by Richard Taylor in a paper entitled "Comments on a Mechanistic Conception of Purposefulness."[3] Taylor points out that to speak of a machine as intending a goal or directing itself toward an end is to speak metaphorically. If, for the sake of argument, such expressions are taken as literally descriptive of machines, the most absurd consequences follow. For example, a machine is described as aiming at a goal if it is geared toward reaching a given coordination in time and space of its parts with certain objects, say, the coincidence of a ship's heading with a given course. At every moment, however, such a coordination of its parts with indefinitely many other objects exists. But such a coordination is, by definition, a goal. Any machine, therefore, aims constantly at an indefinite number of goals. And there is no conceivable way of knowing at which goal, or at which correlation in time and space of machine parts and objects, the machine especially aimed. In fact, all that can properly be said is that the machine parts are correlated at any moment with many objects, and such correlations may, therefore, be taken as just that toward which the machine's behavior was directed. For instance, no matter what the ship's heading, it is on a possible course. Or again, a falling stone at any point of its fall is in spatiotemporal correlation with something and can, therefore, be considered to have been teleologically directed toward that something. At every moment, then, the ship or the stone are achieving their goals, or, in other words, the purpose of the ship or stone, indeed of any object, is to be just where it is at any given moment. This conclusion, however convincing, is a tautology that possesses absolutely no theoretical or explanatory value.

The error of the philosophers who ascribe purpose and teleology to machines lies in their concealing from themselves that they themselves have picked out some one particular coordination of the machine parts with natural objects, as the captain picked out one particular course as the *correct* course. This favored course thus becomes the goal or end. All other courses are wrong and automatically bring the sensing device and output control into play. The machine was designed to achieve just this one particular coordination of heading and course, therefore reaching this goal (coordination) is scarcely extraordinary. But note: there is no "goal" or "end" apart from the captain's selection of the one desired course. The absurdity of supposing the automatic pilot selected its own goal is avoided by confining expressions relating to purpose and pursuit of ends to the meanings they have in common human experience and to derivative uses. Human purposes and values are not to be found in machines or objects considered in themselves; they are to be found in machines and objects only when considered in relation to human or human-derived projects, interests, values. That is, machines or objects have purposes or ends only if they are interpreted as acquiring this function from a source external to themselves. Thus, when we interpret a mechanical system as having a dialectical character in that it moves toward an end, either we speak metaphorically (giving the genus the name of the species, as Aristotle expressed it) or we refer awkwardly to man's use of the mechanical system for his own purposes.

The difficulty into which the authors of "Behavior, Purpose, and Teleology" have plunged themselves is the consequence of failing to attend to the radical distinction between instrument and user, between natural processes and the ends or meanings discovered in, or attributed to, these processes by man. When the development of a geographical area is described as moving toward a mutually sustaining relation of rainfall to vegetation, the teleology that seems to be attributed to this relation is attributed with respect to that particular balance of rainfall to vegetation which men regard as desirable. Nature is then surreptitiously taken as a human artist subtly adjusting means in order to achieve a specific end. Apart, however, from the context of human preferences and values, any relation whatsoever of rainfall to vegetation can be mutually sustaining. To speak of any one such adjustment as more desirable than another is to speak metaphorically. When a torpedo is said to direct itself by the sound of the target ship's propellers or when a cybernetic device is said to keep a ship on its course, we must recall that the apparent teleology involved makes literal sense only within the (human) context of the efficient design and correct use of these machines.

Mechanical dialectic, like natural dialectic, is a metaphorical notion. It refers to work automatically controlled by the difference between the present state of the machine and that which the operator or his superiors regard as the desirable outcome. A human worker may produce a device that works automatically (by negative feedback) toward the end selected by another human worker. Unfortunately, the human user of many of the more complex instruments is often hidden; then the user is easily ignored. For instance, a computer adjusted to use part of its energy searching for a more efficient way of resolving the problem presented to it is still an instrument of the worker who presents the original problem. It may improve, or simplify, as judged by the worker, both the statement of the problem and the original means of solving it; thus, it seems to be independent of the operator. But this appearance is deceptive. My point is that stories of harps that play music by themselves belong to Irish folklore.[4]

Human work, on the other hand, may be described as labor controlled directly by its outcome. I say controlled "directly" for both the sensing device and the output control are intrinsic aspects of the man's human (rational) endowments. This conscious and critical envisagement of the end gives the dialectic an intrinsic direction and a value that are altogether absent in the mechanical process (even when a direction or control is built into a mechanical process). Without this intrinsic sensing device, this evaluation and redirection, the next stage would remain merely a state on a par with any other. In addition, the worker himself is affected by this process. In the course of the work, his envisagement of the goal may change. Likewise, his technique, his manipulation of means to the end, may improve. Thus it could be said that the causality involved in the worker's relation to his work is continuous and mutual; hence, his relation to his work is dialectical. Still, this dialectic is so different from the mechanical causality and "dialectic" discussed earlier that only confusion could result from constantly using the same term for both. Dialectic in its proper and literal sense refers exclusively to human involvements. The mechanical analogies are useful, however, in that they exhibit in simplified form the articulation of the process of continuous reciprocal causality.

The Literal Sense of Dialectic

In addition to the generic and metaphorical senses of dialectic, exemplified in nature and in machines, and to the more familiar and literal sense of dialectic instanced in human work, there are several other species. The distinctions among them may be made by reference to the interpretative contexts within which this dynamic relation is operative. Let us consider three such contexts: interpretation of nature, interpretation of self, and an interaction between interpretation of nature and interpretation of self.

(a) The history of the development of any branch of our knowledge of nature is an objective dialectic in which interpretative theory and observation (ideally) tend toward more perfect correspondence. Thus, the scientist responds to the difference between predictions based upon his theory and his actual observations to measure the adequacy of his theory. When necessary, he introduces changes into his theory to accommodate it more closely to the observed facts. It is as if the scientist inquired of nature whether his theory accurately describes this nature. Nature may respond to this experimental questioning with something like a "yes" or a "no." Some theory, even an incorrect theory provided it is not too far wrong, can guide the student in the collection of data that may suggest a better use of the objective categories and concepts in the construction of an interpretative theory; in turn, this less imperfect theory functions as the guide to the collection of still more exact or more relevant interpretations of experience, and so on. For example, by extending Tycho Brahe's observations of the heavenly bodies made within the context of Brahe's own modification of Copernican-Ptolemaic theory, Johannes Kepler moved toward the discovery of the three laws of planetary motion and contributed to the establishing of Copernican theory. This more adequate theory rendered possible more accurate calculations and predictions, which eventuated in still more precise observations.[5]

The objective dialectic is, of course, more complex than the simple interchange between theory and data. The language of theory (e.g., mathematics), the instruments used in observation and experimentation, and various analogies likewise enter into these relations. For example, a dialectic movement is easy to observe in the development of many scientific instruments. Consider the thermometer. The measure by feeling of hot and cold was rendered more exact by the invention of the mercury thermometer. By use of this instrument the coefficient of expansion of various substances (e.g., glass) when heated could be determined. Knowledge of the coefficient of expansion of glass enabled the experimenter to correct the reading of his thermometer and so to measure temperature to a far greater degree of accuracy and thus to contribute to other improvements in theory and in instruments. Knowledge thus breeds knowledge, as theory and observation correct each other and lead to the development of new and better instruments in a seemingly limitless progress.

(b) Another dialectic utilizing human or existential categories in the interest of self-understanding and of character formation is less easy to characterize. Perhaps Plato's dialogues should be recalled as illustrations; however, I have in mind a dialectic that is rather less intellectualistic than Plato's is usually taken to be. That which is given and is to be interpreted, and so united to the self-aware self, is probably to be identified as the flow of feeling and imagery, particularly the feeling in which one's identity seems especially to be involved. That which affects the interpretation is the store of existential categories and derivative interpretative principles (images, representations, concepts, myths in which the self figures and which each of us has acquired from his culture and developed out of his own past experiences). A primary interpretative principle is the conviction that some degree of freedom of choice is always attainable and that this freedom is sufficient to enable the individual who possesses it to make basic decisions and thus to enter in on the subjective dialectic and eventually to become a self-responsible person.

Natural freedom is the determining gift to the species homo sapiens; in this possession is to be found the difference between man and other animals. By natural freedom I mean liberation from the instincts that care for and guide the other animals at every critical turn of their lives. Instincts are inherited patterns of action; we witness them in the southward flight of geese, in the squirrel's silage, and in the geometry of the spider. Instinct is the internal father of these animals, maintaining them still in their original paradise without responsibility or need of forethought. Evidently instincts were Epimetheus's chief gift to the animals, for without these their other defensive or offensive equipment would be useless. And evidently, too, these instincts were virtually exhausted when he came to endow man. For this reason Prometheus was led to replace them with the fire of intelligence, substituting calculation and prevision for automatisms.

The first fruit of intelligence, as the Greek dramatists conceived it, was a decision on the part of the chief actor, the protagonist, concerning his identity. The middle of a drama was formed by this actor's efforts to live out the identity he had chosen. But these efforts, being made in partial and quite human blindness, seem continually to be about to fail, until the catastrophic moment when the inadequacy of the decision becomes clear for all to see. Even the protagonist himself achieves some insight into the inappropriateness of his initial decision and his failure of self-knowledge. The end of the action is reached in this insight. Here the insight following upon the catastrophic failure of the struggle to embody the initiating decision is something like a measure of the decision and exhibits its inadequacy. Thereupon the table is cleared, so to speak, and readied for a new decision, a new and possibly more adequate output from the protagonist's freedom. Here the "sensing device" is the protagonist's insight into the inadequacy of his initial decision. The "output control" is his reformulation of his decision concerning his identity and function.

According to a humanistic view of man's condition, all of us possess the freedom to enable each to enter in on this dialectical pattern of decision, struggle, catastrophe, and insight. Indeed, all of us are involved in this dramatic dialectic, whether we will or not. This human dialectic is unique. The making of the decision, the evaluation of it in the dramatic insight, the reformulation of it in the initiating decision of the next dramatic action, all are mediated through symbols—language.

Some have seen man's liberation from earlier biological mechanisms mirrored most clearly in his deliberate making and use of symbols as contrasted with the animal's instinctive and mechanical response to signals. The use of human symbols, however, has been attended with almost as much confusion as clarity, and this to such a degree that the human race has sometimes seemed to regret its decision and to wish for a return back to the primal paradise of unconscious art and unthinking self-care, where natural necessities smoothly and efficiently replace confused decisions, halting practice, and failing insight. This atavistic ideal is still very much alive among us, and philosophers from Thomas Hobbes through August Comte to B. F. Skinner have sought to lure men with the image of the perfectly (mechanically) organized and orderly society, where the average man plays only his preassigned role and where the major decisions are made for him. Here every inclination to deviation, every unauthorized expression of individualism, is treated with operant conditioning, drugs, or force. Here we have the peace and order of the machine, the regularity of routine. So far, happily, history has always brought forth a savage, a hero, who could see through the promise of this frozen paradise and could bring others to reject its deadly lure.

Not only dramas of magnitude but also any successful psychiatric session, or even trivial occasions of self-inquiry and self-criticism, exhibit a mutually clarifying and determining relation between the ideals pursued by men and the everyday actualities of human life. Such an interpretation is not merely a means by which feelings and sensations are given meaning and determinateness; the interpreting categories, images, concepts, and myths are clarified at the same time and so become more efficacious in their relation to feeling and sense. The clarification is mutual and developing.

Much of an individual's development may be understood as an effort to render his feelings, emotions, and beliefs more definite and determinate in the interest finally of coming into the unimpeded use of his powers. When, for instance, on a lonely night near a remote and abandoned house a person senses fear, he may well pause and ask just what he is afraid of. He knows nothing overtly dangerous can be lying in ambush. Perhaps, after a modicum of reflection, he concludes that he is merely afraid of being lonely. The fear has thereby become more determinate, less vaguely engulfing, and the person has matured, even though slightly in this instance, in self-understanding and has become more authentically himself. And now, having used his recognition of fear of being lonely as an interpretative principle, he can proceed to ask himself why he should be anxious about loneliness. In what sense is the absence of the other a threat?

No doubt an ideal of the complete and authentic self may be at least remotely envisioned in which all the possibilities of experience have been rendered determinate by this subjective dialectic, leaving no unacknowledged and obscure part of the self remaining in which self-deception and self-doubt may linger to block the using of one's powers—an ideal hardly to be actualized. In many of the more skillfully constructed dramas a movement toward this ideal may be discerned; one thinks immediately of *Oedipus Rex*, of *Antigone*, of *Macbeth*, or of *Murder in the Cathedral*. The property of these dramas that renders them effective lies in the revelatory return of their endings upon their beginnings, measuring and evaluating the latter. When the effect of the action upon the protagonist is sufficiently profound, it tends to turn him back upon his basic views and convictions about himself and his world. Here the sensing device is self-recognition, brought into play by the catastrophe; and here the output control is a reformulation of the decision that initiates another dramatic cycle. Thus, catastrophic action can lead to a revelation of one's deepest persuasions and perhaps to a revision of them. We recall Oedipus' recognition of his overweening self-confidence, Creon's realization of his foolish insistence upon kingly prerogative, Macbeth's insight into his short-sighted and egotistic hunger for power. And we can hardly doubt that any person whatsoever could be caught up in a dialectic that could return him to his primary beliefs (his *archai*) and reveal to him how they are incorporated in a determining fashion in often self-destructive (yet sometimes redeeming) action. This act of being thrown back upon one's basic beliefs I have elsewhere called "archaic experience."[6] It can be exemplified in the life history of movements, of peoples, of cultures, and of individuals. The Cartesian philosophy records such a return, consequent upon the development of the new sciences of the seventeenth century. In our own time, I suggest, the enormous growth of technology, which now threatens to absorb the whole of human life, may invite a catastrophe and a return to basic beliefs and to a reassessment, perhaps a reformulation, of them.

(c) By way of emphasizing this last point I want, finally, to indicate briefly the character of the dialectical relationship that holds between technology and the men concerned with its development, and not with technical men only, but with all men who share in our technological culture.[7]

Once the theory of nature is utilized in the construction of modern labor-saving machines, the technological age has begun. Then men and machines begin a complicated process of interaction and mutual causation of their own. We may call this reciprocal interaction the technological dialectic. An important step in this dialectic occurred when men became aware of the advantages of breaking complex processes down into simple components. The most recent instance is the reduction of thought processes into their simplest components. The accomplishment of this reduction made the computer possible. Technicians have extended this kind of analysis to various fields of activity. Thus, many types of factory work are described in "job descriptions" consisting of accounts of the simplest units into which the whole job may be divided. Apparently complicated jobs are enormously simplified by this procedure. A master workman's complex activity, which probably took him years to learn, can be reduced in this manner to many simple movements, each one of which is easy to learn. A number of workmen (supplemented by machines), each quickly learning and performing a single unit of the simplified tasks, become the equivalent of the master artisan. They do something like the same work far more cheaply and quickly. The outcome is that in most manufacturing the old-fashioned master artisan is no longer needed. Note that complexity has not been eliminated, but now the complexity in the productive process has moved from the master artisan to the organizer and to the technical man. And here, in the organizer and technician, the complexity is more clearly the complexity of the machine. Men and machines, in other words, move toward a state of mutual information, so that it becomes difficult to say whether men have become more mechanical or machines have become more human.

The humanlike character of some of the larger and more modern computers—computers, for example, that are "taught" to play chess so well that they habitually triumph over their teachers—have often been the point of serious and somewhat anxious jokes. Of course, the designers of these machines have had to learn to use computer language and to "think" rather like computers. Furthermore, they recognize the advantages and the cultural need of teaching these languages to the youth. Professors on university faculties have been heard seriously to recommend substituting the teaching of Fortran in place of languages like Greek or French. The sincerity of these professors is evident, although their grasp both upon the nature and function of natural languages and upon the nature and needs of their culture is to be questioned.

In some instances, the human imitation of computers extends well beyond the function of thinking. Social, legal, medical, and even psychiatric problems have been approached as if they were problems for a computer. Programs have been devised that simulate the behavior of experts in some aspects of these fields. Modern social organization also shows the influence of these machines. The thinking done by a carefully structured and well-educated committee, in order to reach a decision about a practical problem, often exemplifies the kind of thinking one expects from a computer. It is as if men were identifying themselves more and more closely with a product of their own collective handiwork. The feedback from efficient machines has been irresistible. Norbert Wiener has remarked that the more we learn about the human brain, the better computers we can construct, and the better computers we construct, the more we can learn about the brain. I do not mean, up to this point, to pass judgment upon this tendency to personal mechanization but merely to take notice of it. Let us now turn to the evaluative step.

The Evaluation of Dialectic

Dialectic is a process, and a process is normally judged by its outcome. In the case of dialectic, however, there are two ways of looking at its outcome. It may be considered intrinsically, as that to which factors internal to the process direct it; or it may be considered extrinsically, as producing an outcome that possesses a value beyond itself. I shall consider here mainly the intrinsic end of a dialectical process.

If we use the term "end" in a metaphorical sense—cf. above, the section "The Generic Sense of Dialectic"—we may identify the intrinsic end of some dialectical processes as their most complex identifiable state. Consider some of the examples already cited. In the cybernetical illustration, the effect of A's causal relation upon B was "fed back" to A, thereby altering A so that its subsequent causal relation to B, as thus changed, would more probably give rise to the B' to which the machine had been adjusted. That is, the accomplishment of dialectic at an earlier stage can function as information directing it to a later state. That which is fed by B back to A is technically called "information." Information relating several physical processes may be regarded as the elements which those processes have in common. The language of this description evidently assumes the partial homogeneity (or the accommodation) of the entities A and B and recalls the prescription of their structural likeness in the quotation from Russell given above. The causal interrelations mediated by "information" gradually move A and B toward the state identified as a goal or end, which is evidently a state in which A and B exhibit a more elaborately developed common structure. Here, as before, the information exchange was mediated through the sensing device and the output control. Consider a biological example. As an animal lives on, its efforts to survive change the environment, and the animal itself becomes changed by this activity, with the result that animal and environment approach a state of mutual adaptation or mutual information; probably the animal or its mutants can then more easily survive in the new environment. The maladaptation of the animal is indicated by its high mortality rate and perhaps also by the production of mutants. The environment reacts, so to speak, by the selection of certain of these mutants for survival. Survival rate is a kind of measure of the animal's adjustment to that environment; selection of better adjusted mutants is like output control. Not only animal and environment but also data and theory, knower and known, actor and that upon which action is directed, can likewise become mutually informed. The data of a theory, for example, may become more and more amply available and increasingly precisely observed as improved theory enables the construction of more selective and accurate instruments. The final and ideal result would be the detailed and complete theory precisely reflecting the whole of the data. And, finally, the human being entertains a dialectical movement between the imaginative and unconscious parts of his psyche and his conscious and rational mind. Probably most physicians would agree that the desirable development requires that both of these parts be closely related; then information, in the healthy mind, will move back and forth between imaginative and unconscious levels of the psyche and the conscious portion of the mind in the form of dreams, reverie, appreciation, and in motor, verbal, and rational activity, with the final consequence that the several parts of the mind become harmoniously related, i.e., "integrated." The conscious and rational mind accepts the imaginative and the unconscious mind, and each reflects the other; the one is constantly translating the enlarging contents of the others into its own economy.

Finally, in the technological dialectic man and machine move through various stages of mutual formation in which machines take over more and more of the functions once performed by humans, and humans come to act more and more with the accuracy and efficiency of machines. Or perhaps, in the event that the nonobjective dialectic be not slighted, machines can be intentionally manipulated so as increasingly to take over the nonhuman tasks in life, thus freeing men to pursue their personal ends and to cultivate their differences from machines. The goal thus indicated, the achievement of identity or similarity of structure, can be accepted as an intrinsic standard and used as a means for passing a rough judgment upon the internal efficiency of dialectical systems. The standard, however, takes more than one form.

It is easy to note, as examples of dialectic are passed in review, that movement toward identity of structure within a dialectical system is of two kinds: finite and continuous. Some dialectical systems achieve a state of equilibrium in which this identity has progressed, apparently, as far as circumstances will allow. When a computing machine solves a problem, it arrives at a definite termination of its designed movement. When a species of animal becomes stabilized within its environment and ceases evolution (e.g., some anthropods), or when a man ceases growth and uses his energy in the repetition of routines, then again the dialectical movement arrives at a (finite) termination. On the other hand, some dialectical contexts do not appear to reach any such point of arrest or routine. The relationship between theory and data in the healthier sciences seems to progress without end toward ever-increasing theoretical precision and scope. Or in a Platonic dialogue, the definitions discovered and the partially solved problems provide instruments and arouse energies for reattacking the same problems and for discovering new ones. Such a dialectical process appears to reach no termination except the continuous clarification of the infinite obscurities in human life and thought, or in the instance of the existential dialectic, a continuous movement toward freedom in the employment of one's powers, and in the instance of the dialectic of nature, a continual growth in theoretical knowledge and in its technological application. In dialectic of the continuous or infinite type, the goal is the continual increase in degree of structural identity or formal similarity among the entities that enter into this relation.

Dialectic moves toward harmonizing the structures of the events that participate in it, but the harmony actually achieved may not always be that which is desired by someone using a dialectical process. For this reason, in part at least, dialectic has acquired a bad name among some philosophers. The only standard intrinsic to dialectic, however, seems to be the standard relative to the movement toward similarity in form or identity of structure among the events that participate in it. A dialectical process is intrinsically good if the events involved in it do in fact move through mutual interaction toward increasing similarity in form. Whether the form is that which is desired by someone making use of the process for his own ends can be decided only by reference to criteria external to the dialectic itself.

Is there ever any reason to expect any dialectical process to reach a final end that ought to be regarded as unqualifiedly good? The answer to this question—human prejudice to one side—must depend upon the nature of the principles the thinker is able to bring to bear upon the problem and upon the final values, usually expressed in myths or world symbols, intended to justify those principles. The task, though, of discovering the myths actually accepted by a people and used to provide the final defense for its categories of value opens up quite another pursuit. The present point is restricted to this: the intrinsic end of a dialectical development is homogeneity of structure of the events composing it. But dialectic cannot propose its external end; this end must be selected for it. Once, though, the end or specific type of identity of structure is proposed and incorporated in a dialectical system by suitable means, or made intrinsic to it, the process may move toward its achievement.

In the instance of a mechanical or technological dialectic, I tried to show that the end must always be externally imposed and that an intrinsic end is an end only in a metaphorical sense. The human being, however, may propose ends in the proper sense and contrive to impose them upon a dialectical process.

Undeniably, many dialectical movements have advanced to unforeseen and catastrophic conclusions in defiance of the criteria applied. The course of events that swept an Oedipus or a Macbeth on to their ends can scarcely be imagined to have been explicitly proposed by them. Rather, they were moved inexorably on to the intrinsic end of a vaguely grasped dialectic. In the larger sense, however, the sense in which any man may be thought to desire to be himself, these heroes may be said to have willed their unhappy histories, for thus they came further to know and to be themselves. A more determined and perhaps a more sophisticated hero might have designed, or at least have acquiesced in, such a series of events had there been a reasonable assurance of moving through them into self-knowledge. He would thus have willed his own fate, and he would have judged the dialectical process so designed by an external standard: its effectiveness in leading him to self-knowledge. Such a protagonist is possessed of *amor fati* and is by way of becoming an authentic person.

Perhaps, though, the operations of a beneficent fate cannot always be relied upon to guide the movement of dialectic toward the human good. We may suspect that dialectic helps those who help themselves by an exercise of foresight and self-guidance. We should, therefore, anticipate that the experience of one involved in the mutually causal relations between man and modern machines, a technological dialectic, is caught in a movement toward the intrinsic end of this dialectic, and this end is the accommodation or similarity of man and machine. Those locked in the progress of this dialectic must, therefore, expect the growing homogeneity between men and machines to gain momentum in their own personal development, with the consequence that mechanical routines, not their own individual styles of existing, become the end product. For *amor fati* they inevitably tend to substitute an *amor machinae*. That machines should communicate their properties, their routines, to men seems an unhappy issue from this relationship. For if men are indeed radically different from machines, then their efforts to become mechanical, just that which they are not, cannot but be followed by frustration and unhappiness. Important to consider, then, is the possibility that the technological dialectic of man and machine should be made to conform to some extrinsic standard more favorable to humankind and its growth. Is such a determination possible and desirable? Thereby hangs a long argument.[8]

Communication:
Technology and Ethics

Henry W. Johnstone, Jr.

It is difficult to draw a line between technological and non-technological aspects of human behavior.[1] There is a sense in which everything we do falls under the rubric of technology. If technology embraces every use of a tool, it embraces everything; for unless tools be restricted to physical implements, tool use is ubiquitous in human life. A language is as much a tool as is a hammer, and the use of language is as much technology as is driving a nail. Social and political organization can likewise be construed as technological. Perhaps we will want to insist on a distinction between technological and purely natural activities, but the latter are difficult to find. Man has no nature; he has only technology.

Yet not much is accomplished by permitting this extension of the concept of the technological. If everything man does answers to a technology, we still need to distinguish technologies that make us feel threatened from those we feel should be fostered. It is my purpose to make this distinction in one way. I shall argue that the technologies that are substituted for creativity are felt as a threat to human communication. My discussion will be in effect a sketch of one aspect of the technology in the ordinary sense that is subject to such radical generalization.

My task is now to explain both the distinction I am making between technology of a certain kind and creativity, and the conditions under which I regard communication as creative. The distinction in question is often made, but I repeat it in order to approach the relatively unfamiliar concept of creative communication. Creativity, in the sense in which I am using the term here, is a property of certain processes. A process is creative if it consists of a series of steps none of which is strictly determined either by the project that the steps contribute to or by the preceding steps in the series, but each of which, once taken, is seen to have been a fitting sequel to its predecessors. One example of such a process is the one in which I am engaged as I write this paper. My sentences do not determine their successors, and my project as a whole does not determine my sentences. Yet I hope that these new sentences I write will be appropriate to those that have gone before; that this one, for example, will be appropriate. Sometimes I succeed too well; my sentences build so tightly upon their predecessors that I cannot pry them apart to insert new material that may have occurred to me as an afterthought. It is always painful to me to have to rewrite what I have written, because my sentences seem to form a tissue that is difficult to alter without destroying it altogether.

A simpler example of the sort of process I am calling "creative" is the art of arrangement. Flowers, furniture, and writings can be arranged in sequences in which the placement of no item is determined by its predecessors or by the project as a whole, yet the placement of each is fitting. Thus the arrangement of the odes of Horace is such that a critic can admit that "Horace himself might have produced a dozen different groupings on a dozen different days."[2] I take this to mean that even beginning where he did begin—with an obligatory ode dedicating his book to his patron—Horace might have proceeded in a variety of ways and that in each of these ways he would have produced a sequence of odes each somehow appropriate to its predecessors. I will not pause long over the objection that when all but one of the odes have been chosen, the order of the last one is determined. This presupposes that the process is strictly linear. Clearly, however, Horace was able to look ahead and pick out in advance the ode that he wanted to be the last.

Notice the retrospective judgments forced on us by a creative process. We cannot decide in advance what item will be the most fitting sequel to a given sequence. Only when an item is in place can we judge it.

Having tried to suggest a sense of "creativity," let me now try to suggest a sense of "technology" in which the products of technology contrast with the products of creativity. A process is technological in this sense when it is a series of steps in which either a given step or the project as a whole determines the sequel to the given step or else the question whether the successor is fitting to its predecessors does not arise. Consider a trip from State College, Pennsylvania, my home town, to Ann Arbor, Michigan. I have planned the whole of this trip in advance. I know in what direction I must start. I know that in a certain predetermined place—namely, Woodland, Pennsylvania—I must turn westward on I-80. At Toledo, I must turn north on U.S. 23. It is important to be clear about the meaning of "must" as I have just used it. I am not saying that the route I have chosen is the only route from State College to Ann Arbor. Indeed, there are a very large number of them; there is, as they say, more than one way to skin a cat. I mean simply that with the aid of a map I have chosen the segments of my trip in advance. These segments are determined by my plan. But clearly not all of them would be included in everyone's plan. My plan itself is determined by the desire to take the shortest route; someone else might wish to stop in Pittsburgh on the way, and so would plan differently.

I am speaking here of what Kant called "counsels of prudence" and sometimes "technical imperatives."[3] He clearly stated that the means are determined by the end in such cases.

Of course, a trip as a whole can be a step in a creative

process. Perhaps my trip is the product of an impulse that could not have been foreseen. We would then have to ask whether the trip was in some way appropriate to the episodes upon which it ensued. If so, we could regard the entire process as creative.

A trip might also be creative in its own right. If its segments were not determined by a plan, and yet each was appropriate to its predecessors, we might think of the trip as constituting genuine travel. For a travel is precisely a creative trip,[4] a trip for which we could not have accounted in advance but each segment of which is a fitting outcome of previous segments. Thus I might find myself in Ann Arbor as the result of a pursuit that led me there unpredictably. Perhaps the thought of going there arose only during the course of a more extended journey. If my going makes sense in the light of my entire journey, the trip would seem to qualify as a travel. A noncreative trip, on the other hand, is an errand, although of course the process that constitutes the purpose of the errand may be creative. Perhaps creativity of some sort awaits me once I get to Ann Arbor.

The point of all these remarks is that creativity may be inextricably involved with technology. It is not always easy or even possible to separate them from each other.

Why do I associate noncreative processes with technology? It seems to me typical of projects requiring tools (in the narrow sense of "tool" in which only a material object can be one) that each step in the project determines the next, or the project itself determines the entire sequence of steps. Thus if my project is to build a box, and my tools are ruler, saw, hammer, and nails, I must measure, saw, and nail boards in one of a certain number of fixed orders—the end determines the means. To be sure, I am free to choose whether to make the left or right side first, but whatever order I do choose fixes in advance the relationship among all the steps. If my project is to get to Ann Arbor, and my tools are a car, a system of

highways, and a map, once again I fix in advance the relationships among the steps. Of course, there may be a detour
or a traffic tieup ahead that I can skirt by altering my route.
Such problems are like the problems posed when my wood
splits or I find that my nails are too short. They call for a
revision of the project. Once it is revised, the steps are again
fixed in advance as they were before. Technological projects
of this kind are quite distinct from Horace's project of arranging his odes.

Of course, in the extended sense of "tool," Horace did have
tools; he used language, for example. But his project did not
determine his use of his tools. The project of building a box
requires specific uses of a saw, but no specific deployment of
language is presupposed by the project of arranging odes.

Let me summarize my understanding of the narrow sense
of "technology," a sense I am contrasting with creativity.
Technology in this sense requires tools that are material objects and is a property of processes in which a series of steps is
determined by the project that the steps, taken together, are
intended to accomplish, or in which individual steps are determined by their predecessors. I should suppose that technology in this narrow sense could arise only when both these
conditions—i.e., that of tool use and that of determination of
means by end—are met. One could, for example, have tool
use without determination, as in the work of some artists. On
the other hand, the conditions I have stated are probably not
exhaustive. There are projects I would not classify as technological—certain art projects, for example—in which the
steps are determined by the project.

I turn now to creative communication. According to my
previous definition, a communicative process is creative if it
consists of a series of steps none of which is strictly determined by its predecessors but each of which, once taken, is
seen to have been a fitting sequel to its predecessors. The
steps are obviously speeches; the process as a whole is

obviously a dialogue. And indeed the dialogue is precisely the form of communication in which no speech is determined in advance but each is seen, in retrospect, as somehow appropriate to its predecessors. I want to note one salient feature of this form of communication, namely, that two or more people are cooperating; taking turns to make the step that is retrospectively seen to be appropriate. This is not like the task of Horace, for example, who himself took all the steps.

Creative communication fulfills a condition I once specified for fruitful philosophical discussion: it is "bilateral."[5] In a bilateral discussion one interlocutor does not aim to prevent the other from using all the techniques and arguments that he (the first interlocutor) uses. To do so would be to attempt to block the response of the other. But this is precisely what a cooperative activity would avoid.

I do not specify how many steps a dialogue must contain. Two are enough. Even a single speech might count as a dialogue if it opened the possibility of a response that was not actually forthcoming.

Let us ask what dialogue is good for. Can dialogue have results yielded by no other process? This question has been dealt with extensively in literature I prefer not to examine here. I propose only to suggest what implications my distinction between the technological and the creative might have for this question. For one unique advantage of dialogue will emerge if we consider what would be lost if all communication were technological.

There are small computers that play chess. A game against the computer is a good example of a process at least half of which is technological, for the computer's moves are determined by its program. Thus each of its steps depends upon all the preceding steps. It is, of course, possible to beat the machine—especially if one has switched it to a low enough level of performance. But I wonder if beating the machine isn't similar in principle to beating a machine of another kind—the box containing holes in which a set of balls are to be lodged, i.e., the hand-held prototype of the pinball machine. One wins that game by manipulating the box with skill of a certain kind. Doesn't one also win the game of chess by manipulating a box in a certain way? To be sure, the two sorts of manipulation are different. One is manual, the other a matter of mastering sequences of buttons to push; a matter, in effect, of mastering its program. But in the end, winning the game of chess is just a sophisticated version of putting the balls in the holes. And once this goal is achieved, the process is wholly technologized. The human player can claim that *he* takes steps determined by the antecedent steps of the process in which he is engaged. Meanwhile, the machine's half of the game is no longer seen as a series of steps at all. It is simply a sequence of states, each determined by the person's moves. The machine has ceased to function as a person and thus has ceased to present itself as a being capable of exercising technology. For the human player, on the other hand, playing chess is as much like building a box as it is like putting balls in holes. For responding to a move of the machine is like making a necessary measurement or driving a necessary nail. It is the person alone who exercises the technology of chess play.

To test my own phenomenological expectations as expressed here, I acquired a chess machine when I was writing this essay. At first, my games with my machine seemed to disconfirm these expectations. For I could not distinguish the machine's program from its chess play. I was, in other words, playing against it as a person, not as a program. Later, however, I came to realize that a better chess player than I would have no difficulty in distinguishing program from play. This would have to be true at least of the person who had written the program.

I am not trying to suggest that there is anything inaccurate about describing chess play as a technology. Winning moves are winning moves, whether played against a machine or against a human opponent. But there is a difference between the phenomenology of engineering a chess game with a machine and that of playing chess with another person. One way of suggesting what I have in mind is to consider what would have happened at the Iceland tournament if Bobby Fischer had been a machine. Would Boris Spassky then have lost? There is, of course, no way of knowing. We are told that, over and over again, Spassky was "psyched out" by Fischer. I doubt, however, that Spassky could have been "psyched out" by a machine.

"Psyching out" is one of the cruder versions of a result we might expect from creative communication but not from technological communication. It represents a certain zero level of creative communication, an enormous refusal under minimal conditions of cooperation. This I will now try to show.

I remarked earlier that dialogue is a form of cooperation. Each interlocutor makes a response that he hopes the others will see as appropriate to what has gone before, even though this response may well consist of the denial of the previous speech. A denial can, of course, be fully as appropriate or inappropriate as a speech of any other kind; when it is appropriate, it is seen by each interlocutor as an act of cooperation. Clearly, you can cooperate with me by opposing me as well as you can by agreeing with me. But this would be cooperation at a far higher level than the minimum cooperation of the psych-out.

Because he did not regard Bobby Fischer as a machine, Boris Spassky expected that Fischer's responses to his moves would constitute a cooperative endeavor to maintain the game as a tissue of appropriate moves. And in the minimal way I have in mind, his expectations were fulfilled. Bobby Fischer indulged in no illegal conduct during the course of his games; according to the book, his responses were entirely appropriate, not only as legal chess moves but also as pieces of behavior perfectly consistent with the professional decorum of the game. What he did to upset Spassky can perhaps not be fully described in an objective way. To be sure, he canceled games and haggled over conditions. Perhaps what really counted, though, is that he simply seemed to radiate baleful energy, to sit as a malignant presence at his side of the board. If so, this was a radical refusal to cooperate in the context of an outward conformity that was minimal.

Spassky would clearly have been better off to regard Fischer as a machine. He got into trouble because two conditions were met at once. In the first place, he regarded Fischer as a person, thus harboring certain expectations about the kind of cooperation he would get from Fischer. In the second place, when these expectations were disappointed he could not simply revert to the hypothesis that Fischer was after all a machine incapable of cooperating in a personal way. He was already caught up in a personal encounter and could only see Fischer as *refusing* to cooperate. It was no doubt the refusal that psyched him out. People respond to the incapacity of machines to cooperate not by being psyched out but in other ways, which I will try to describe in due course.

If we should meet a figure disembarking from a flying saucer, we might expect cooperation at some level. This expectation might be disappointed in two ways. On the one hand, the figure might, on closer inspection, turn out to be not the sort of object of which cooperation could be asked. Perhaps it is only an Earth probe engineered to collect samples of our soil and transmit information about them to a distant monitor. On the other hand, the figure might *refuse* to cooperate. Why, after all, *should* a being of superior intelligence cooperate with moronic earthlings? Why not simply dominate them? But I suspect that if an alien race came to master us it would be difficult for us at first to dispel the notion that our visitors were machines. He who would master must first be taken seriously; he must somehow reveal himself as a person.

As I write, in late December 1979, there are examples of

refusals to cooperate in places closer to home, specifically in Iran. We take the refusers seriously; we regard them as human persons. Our inability to regard them as machines has contributed to our ineffectuality in dealing with the crisis in Iran.

There are now two topics I want to discuss. First, what are the ethical implications of the cooperation that is integral to creative communication? Second, what threat is technological communication perceived as posing? I have mentioned the threat of the psych-out, but I have yet to consider how a machine can threaten us once it is exposed as a machine. The danger that exists when a machine threatens us, it will turn out, is even greater than the danger of the psych-out.

If I were to judge in terms of some already accepted ethical theory the various moves called for in creative communication, those of my readers who do not happen to hold the ethical theory I use as a touchstone would have a right to protest. So I am not going to try to vindicate dialogue, as I perceive it, on Utilitarian, Kantian, or Intuitionistic grounds. Instead I want to see what ethical theory, if any, flows naturally from my analysis of dialogue. If, as I foresee, the theory that emerges bears some resemblance to Kantianism, it is important to understand that this is the resemblance of members of the same race, not that of parent and child.

Let us return to the psych-out. I have called it "one of the cruder versions of a result we might expect from creative communication but not from technological communication." In what way is the psych-out crude? In a certain way it corresponds to a very primitive level of personal existence—primitive historically and primitive in personal development. The dialogue of Homeric heroes consists partly of attempts to psych one another out; witness the quarrel between Achilles and Agamemnon on which the plot of the *Iliad* turns, a quarrel in which each disputant is trying, without success, to overmaster his antagonist by his sheer presence or "antecedent ethos"; the words he uses are almost irrelevant. And the child experiences parental psych-out as part of a normal upbringing.

My point is that the pure psych-out is at the lower end of a continuum of responses to the demands of creative communication. Though crude, it is a personal response, not that of a machine. All of us, including Spassky, perceive its perpetrator as a person. Dialogue occurs only among persons. Persons, for that matter, require dialogue. The only alternatives to creative communication are technological communication and no communication at all. And technological communication is in fact only an unstable phase of a transition that leads to no communication at all. If I so exclusively occupy myself with playing chess with a machine that I end up simply manipulating it in order to win, clearly I am no longer communicating with it. If I am surrounded by machines, whether they are designed to communicate or not, not only do I get no cooperation but nothing calls for my own cooperation. In other words, there will be no occasion for me to exhibit my own humanity. It is probable that under such circumstances a person could not survive indefinitely as a person. His environment would sooner or later brutalize him. From the role of sole technological manipulator of the machines around him he would pass to the final phase of his degradation; he would become a machine himself, a machine interacting with other machines in a minuet of meaningless transfers of energy. He would have turned from a specimen of *homo faber* into one of what Jürgen Habermas calls *"homo fabricatus."*[6] Perhaps it is this possibility that Thoreau had in mind when he complained that "men have become the tools of their tools."[7]

That a person might not actually undergo this degradation in a lifetime—that, like Robinson Crusoe, he might emerge unscathed from his cave after several decades of solitary existence—is irrelevant. The disvalue of degradation is not refuted by anyone's physiological capacity to withstand it. Simi-

larly, to choose another example, the capacity of an unde-
tected murderer to survive for many years without the slightest remorse is no argument against the appropriateness of
such remorse.

We are moving from fact to obligation—from the *is* to the
ought. This is always a difficult move; the motive force is
likely to be that of fallacy. So watch my argument closely. I
want to contend that since the solitary life of a person among
machines is a disvalue, posing as it does the threat that the
person might himself become a machine, it will be imperative
for a person to seek out other persons and contribute to their
status as persons. He can do this only by engaging in dialogue, by tendering to others the cooperation he needs from
them if his own status as a person is to be nurtured and
enhanced. The rule he must follow is "Respond to the
speeches of others in such a way that your response, while not
determined by the dialogue, is yet appropriate to its previous
steps." Another version of this rule is "So act as to treat all
humanity, whether in your own person or in that of another,
as a person, not as a machine only; i.e., treat yourself and any
other person as primarily an agent capable of cooperating in a
dialogue."

It is only fair to point out that the second version extends
somewhat the notion of a dialogue. Beginning as it does with
the imperative "So act . . ." it refers not just to speeches but
to actions of all sorts. Two points, however, are clear. First,
an ethics of speeches alone would not be a complete ethics,
because many acts that require moral evaluation are not acts
of speaking. Second, the dialogue model can very easily be
adapted to accommodate acts of all kinds. We need only
imagine a cooperative enterprise involving acts each of which,
though not determined by the enterprise, is appropriate to its
previous steps.

What would exemplify such an enterprise? I have already
taken the liberty of using one example—the game of chess

among persons, which does not, after all, require speech acts. One must communicate with a chess machine, but one's behavior in playing chess with a person does not require that one *communicate* one's moves to him; one simply *makes* moves. Nearly any game, in fact, would exemplify the enterprise I have in mind. Among games that would not are ones that can be forced to a win or a draw from the beginning— such as nim and checkers—because in such games at least half the moves are determined in advance, as are the moves of a chess machine.

Nor is there any reason why the examples must be restricted to games. Action in a social setting is a creative enterprise, from which an ethics flows. To be sure, action usually is accompanied by communication at a more or less explicit level, but it need not be. The acts involved in driving a car are creative; we are warned that we can never be sure what the other driver will do, but we hope that it will be appropriate. A traffic violation, furthermore, is perceived in our culture as an ethical lapse, not merely a violation of our civil code. For American society puts an emphasis on cooperative driving which at other times and places has been put on chivalry or good citizenship. The accident-causer is a pariah.

What I am saying has consequences that can be dealt with only in an essay ten times the length of this one. It is easy to think of cases that seem to violate the rule I have stated. Clearly, there are times when it is necessary, and ethically right, to treat another as if he were a machine; one shouts at another, attempting to engage his reflexes, to get him to jump out of the way of an oncoming vehicle; one deals with a wayward child by force. The issue then is whether we have treated the other as a machine *only*. If not, it is still arguable that the act was right.

But my emphasis must be on communication, because this concept rather than action in general is a theme in the continuing colloquium to which I am attempting to contribute. Clearly, my rule in either of its versions defines an ethics of communication. And equally clearly, any violation of these rules is an ethical lapse. The rubric under which all such violations fall is that of uncreative behavior when creative communication is called for. It is important, however, to be sure that my readers understand under what conditions I assert that a communicative act is uncreative. A performance making use of a certain degree of force is not necessarily uncreative. Thus even the psych-out can contribute to a dialogue of sorts. However much people may deplore Bobby Fischer's treatment of Boris Spassky, they do not deplore this treatment on ethical grounds. Fischer was not, in any event, treating Spassky like a machine. At a very primitive and crude level he was unleashing forces of persuasion. One persuades a person, not a machine. Persuasion is clearly a dimension of dialogue. In dialogue, any appropriate move must be persuasive; if it is not, this is because a gap is perceived in its appropriateness.

Among communicative acts most emphatically in violation of the ethics of communication is the act of putting another person on hold. To place another on hold is not only to treat him as an object incapable of making a creative response; it is to force him into a position in which he can make no response whatever. The violation is all the more heinous because it is a machine, in all probability, that has put the person on hold. This is a machine he cannot hope to manipulate; it will simply keep him on hold until the line clears. All hope for dialogue collapses.

I want to argue that all technological communication results in placing the human partner on hold. I have suggested that this is the outcome of play with a chess machine; for, once the illusion of an opposing player vanishes and one is simply manipulating the box, no creative response is possible. As the player himself becomes absorbed into the system of buttons he is less and less able to make any response. His preoccupation has depersonalized him.

The moral indignation of a person put on hold often takes

the form of anger. Anger under such circumstances is salutary, for it is the response of a person who cannot respond otherwise. The one who plays a chess machine ought to express anger, but it is too late; once he has been deprived of the power to respond, anger is no longer a possibility for him.

An evangelist once told the more hesitant members of an audience he was addressing, "God has put you on hold." His was an unloving God. It is possible to feel these days, however, that the Universe has put us on hold, especially when machines are on the way to becoming our only access to the Universe. It is not only the telephone and the chess machine that put us on hold, but all computerized channels of information and some that are not computerized. In some cases, to be sure, we escape being put on hold because we do not think we are called on to respond creatively, for example, when we obey traffic signals. When we are sufficiently meek, we do not risk being depersonalized.

I began by narrowing the focus of my inquiry to technology that uses tools that are material objects. The chess machine and the telephone are such tools. The Greek word for "tool" is "organon." Clearly, Aristotle (or his ancient editors) did not conceive of his *Organon* as a tool that was a material object— they did not, for example, think of it as a logic machine. It is nonetheless interesting that Aristotle's *Rhetoric* falls outside the scope of his *Organon*; rhetoric is not a tool even in an extended sense. Perhaps what I have said in this paper will help to suggest why rhetoric is not a tool. Fischer's psych-out of Spassky was rhetoric in a very primitive form; it was persuasion at a crude level. Yet it served to distinguish Fischer from a machine. Machines do not engage in persuasion because persuasion is a creative move. An attempt to persuade is a move not determined by a dialogue but seen as appropriate to the previous speeches of the dialogue. Persuasion is in fact, to my way of thinking, a modality of speaking to which all other steps in creative communication may be reduced. For it is the one modality that no use of tools can wholly replace. A machine may inform me what the result of applying a complex mathematical formula to a set of data is; when it does, I am perfectly willing to accept the information, feeling that it has come from an appropriate source. A machine can give me current stock market quotations. It can tell me that I owe $265.00 for airline tickets. But it cannot persuade me to pay that amount, even if it uses strong language, unless I perceive behind it a human programmer framing the message in an effort to get me to pay.

I make this point about the status of persuasion in order to create a link between this paper and another recent one.[8] In that effort, I took persuasion to be definitive of man's nature. I tried then to develop a moral rule basically requiring the maintenance of this nature. The rule I developed was not much different from my present one, which I will now repeat: "So act as to treat all humanity, whether in your own person or in that of another, as a person, not as a machine only."

The Technological Embodiment of Media

Don Ihde

The simplest and purest notion of a communication relation between individuals might be characterized as a "face-to-face" relation. It would be akin to John Dewey's notion of the simplest school—two individuals, each seated on the end of a log, conversing with one another uninterrupted and unimpeded. A simple dialogue between two individuals exemplifies such a communication situation. Whatever complexities might arise would relate only to the two speakers. Thus, clear, honest, and straightforward communication could be impeded in that one or the other speaker might dissemble, lie, exaggerate, or use any of the many possible devices humans use to hide from or fool each other. Nevertheless, the face-to-face situation allows for the possibility of authentic, truthful, and open communication.

What happens, then, when this direct communication situation is varied such that the situation is no longer that of two individuals seated on their respective log ends; when the situation is one in which the communication must take place through some third element, a medium? Factually and familiarly, this second situation is becoming more and more commonplace and is simply taken for granted by most of us in advanced technological society. What day does not go by without the use of the telephone—a common medium; or when we do not listen to the radio or television for anything from entertainment to getting vital news and information; or when do we not pick up a newspaper, magazine, or book as yet another genre of media taken for granted?

That communication occurs by means of media is such a commonplace that we rarely reflect, let alone reflect critically, upon the implication of what I shall call a "third factor" in the communication situation. We are, furthermore, quite aware that all of the possibilities that can occur in the face-to-face situation to create complexities and distortions of communication can also occur with the use of media—lies, dissembling, covering over things are just as possible with media as they are with humans face to face. And because this is so, we might be tempted simply to assume that everything that is possible in the face-to-face situation occurs in a "mediated" situation—and in some sense it does. But we might also be tempted in this assumption to overlook a whole dimension of interesting phenomena that are unique to the "mediated" communication situation.

It is here that I shall strike the theme for this investigation: what role do media play in the situation of human communication? Does the introduction of such "third factors" as media change or in any way transform the communication situation? And, if so, how? My inquiry, then, is a *phenomenology of media* with particular focus upon the experience of media in concrete communication situations. My general argument will seek to demonstrate that there is a unique way in which the introduction of media—communications technologies—transforms the communication situation. This transformation of the communication situation, I shall argue, is both inevitable (a necessary condition) and nonneutral (transformational) with respect to any communication situation that utilizes communications technologies.[1] A phenomenology, as an inquiry into these phenomena, directs itself to uncovering what might be called invariant or essential features of such situations and in the process begins to unravel somewhat broader implications for the overall human impact of technology.

To accomplish this task I shall take the following steps:

First, I shall examine some of our usual ways of looking at things with a concern for habits that cause us to overlook important features of our experience of things. What might be called the impact of communications technologies upon human experience is often simply overlooked, and, if not overlooked, might not be isolated with sufficient clarity to merit its own investigation. Second, I shall introduce in brief and simple terms some of the key phenomenological notions which I shall employ in undertaking a thematic study of the communication situation. And third, I shall analyze a series of common media-embodied communication situations to point up and isolate the specifically invariant features of the technological transformation of human communication.

Technologies of Communication

First, I take a brief look at certain temptations that cause us to overlook the unique effects of technologies upon our communication experience. What has become known as the electronic communications revolution began earlier in the century. Older media, such as print in all of its forms, have been with us for some centuries, but the newer media, embodied in electronics technologies, began to allow the human voice to be carried to distances never possible for even the most imaginable shouting match. One such early invention was the transatlantic telephone cable. With it Edison's Watson could be heard not just in a nearby room, but across the Atlantic. But problems emerged: the very machinery that was to transmit the sound of the voice created its own noise that was also transmitted. Indeed, after certain distances, the voice of the machinery (amplifiers and the like) literally "covered over" the sound of the voice that was supposed to be transmitted. Here, one could clearly claim, the technology being employed was nonneutral in an obviously negative sense. It intruded into the very purpose of the system, which was to convey an understandable human speech. Something had to be done to impede the machinery-produced noise and to enhance the desired sound, that of the voice, if the communication were to occur at all. That is, the transmission must *embody* the conversation "transparently" and not itself intrude into the communication situation.

We, of course, know the outcome of this early communications technology problem. We can now telephone practically anyone in far-reaching places of the world and hear them as clearly as, or better than, the earlier technologies allowed us to hear persons in the next village. (We have even replaced the cable with satellite.) Experientially, some degree of hoped-for "transparency" of communication has been achieved. Although not all noise of transmission has been removed, it is now no more than background to the foreground of technologically mediated human speech.

In this example, however, the nonneutrality of technology as it embodies human communication has been noted negatively. Insofar as transmission noises intrude into the mediated communication situation, they impede and restrict that communication. This apparent negativity, however, can also be inverted as in the famous example developed by Martin Heidegger in his analysis of our use of equipment, specifically tools. His example was the use of a simple hammer.[2] The user of a hammer, he points out, does not focus upon or relate to the hammer in the work situation. Rather, when the hammer is functioning in the use situation, it is the work—that upon which the human using the hammer works—that is experienced. In such use situations the hammer "withdraws" or becomes "transparent" as the very condition of its usefulness. This is a positive feature in the use of a technology that allows us to perform otherwise unperformable tasks. Similarly, when we make a long distance telephone call, the instrument and its associated and very complex equipment experientially "recede" and we focus upon and experience the conversation with the other. In short, when the technology is good—at least in this kind of use situation—it becomes semitransparent with respect to communication. It can be functionally "forgotten." Conversely, only when it functions poorly or does not work at all does it obtrude itself into our experiential aims. A measure of the quality of this type of technology is in fact the degree of "transparency" it may allow the user.

The extension of this observation for communication situations is clear enough—those media that most enhance "transparency" will be seen in some sense to be superior to those that obtrude into the communication situation. The clear sounding telephone system that allows me to recognize the individual voice of the other is obviously superior to one that makes the other sound so "phony" and "tinny" that he or she is a mere generalized other. And if this degree of auditory transparency is best when maximized, can we not anticipate even more adequate forms of more global transparencies? Should we not move toward the television-telephone that would allow us to see as well as hear the other? I shall return to this later, but at the moment I wish to take account of two temptations that pose themselves at this juncture of the inquiry.

We have now recognized that for a technology to function well, it must itself become a barely noticed background effect. It must itself "withdraw" so that the human action that is embodied through the technology can stand out. This "withdrawal" or "transparency," however, simultaneously poses two temptations that can make us forget certain essential features of the mediated communication situation.

First, if the better the technology is the more it becomes transparent, could we not hope for and aim toward what I shall call the *perfectly transparent* situation? Could we not have a technology that was so perfect that we could not notice it at all? This is what I shall call the idealization of a technology. There are two interesting aspects to this temptation: first, what would the perfectly transparent technology allow? Obviously, a nonmediated communication situation, one in which the technology was so transparent that it would be invisible and thus equivalent to being a nontechnologically mediated situation. In short, this is an idealized reduction to the simplest communication situation, the face-to-face situation that is not technologically mediated.

The dreamer who wishes for the perfectly transparent technology thus secretly harbors a wish for no technology at all—or at least its equivalent. The dreamer would like to be face to face with the other. But this does not occur with actual technologies, because no matter how relatively transparent they become, they remain far from perfect transparency. But I am pointing out here what I regard as a deep ambivalence in the idealizer: there is simultaneously a wish for certain things a technology can give us, for example, the long distance communication which the long distance telephone gives us, and a wish that the technological embodiment be functionally nontechnological or direct. In short, this is something like a wish to be godlike.

If the first temptation opens a direction toward the idealization of technological possibilities, the second temptation allows us to forget the subtle presence of a technology as a "third element" in mediated communication situations.

A "good" technology, we have seen, does not call attention to itself; it "withdraws" in use. And the better it functions, the more likely it becomes that we may simply grow used to its functions and "forget" that it is there and that it is a significant element in our now mediated communication situation. We take the technology for granted in such a way that we increasingly disregard its presence. We allow whatever is unique to the mediated communication situation to be forgotten or covered over. But what if the use of a technology, any technology, is essentially nonneutral? What if such uses transform human experience and communication in fundamental ways? Should we not then become aware of and reflective about such transformations? Put positively, should we not attempt to reflect critically and deeply about the ways we communicate in such technologically embodied situations?

At this juncture, I wish to turn to a more analytic description and begin to develop a phenomenology of communications technologies.

A *Phenomenology*

I begin by very briefly and simply taking note of a few major conclusions phenomenologists have drawn about the shape of human experience. I then move directly into an elementary application of these notions to a simple communication situation before proceeding to more complex variations.

The key notion used by phenomenologists to interpret experience is called *intentionality*. This term contains a multiplicity of meanings, but designates primarily a certain "shape" of experience. What is claimed is that all human experience is directed—it is selective and focused upon an experienced environment which we shall call *world*. A world is an experiential space and time that is simultaneously present to us and yet in some sense "other than" and "distant" from us. I shall formalize this first characterization of intentionality as follows:

Human————————————→ World

Here the "human" is the experiencer and the "world" is the environment that is experienced. The arrow signifies the involved focus of experience as it is directed toward "world." We have here, then, a primitive theory of action—I am primarily a being who acts toward and within a world (and action in the phenomenological sense includes even perceptual acts, indeed, in some sense these are basic).

This directed, actional involvement with a world is not only one-directional, however, it is also reflexive or interactive. Phenomenology interprets intentionality not only as a distance from and involvement in world, but as reflexive with respect to world. This is to say that the shape of our experience is such that, at bottom, what we eventually come to know of ourselves is strictly reciprocal with what we come to know of the world.[3] Without world there would be no self; without self, no experience of world. The reflexive structure of intentionality, then, can be signified by noting the way world is taken back into my self-experience with a second arrow making intentionality interactive:

$$\text{Human} \rightleftharpoons \text{World}$$

These illustrations point up a minimal set of operative notions from phenomenology that can now be applied to the inquiry into the experience of media. What remains is to isolate and delimit the inquiry so as to detect the salient features of the transformations of experience which media make possible. In so doing I wish to introduce a technical interpretation of what shall count as a medium for purposes of this essay: A medium, as I use it here, includes (a) some material artifact that is experientially used in a particular way to (b) convey what may be called broadly an expressive activity. Thus the ordinary sense of media, such as newspapers, radio, cinema, television, will be preserved because in each case an artifact or set of artifacts (technologies) are used to convey information and messages and to entertain, stimulate, or arouse.

Such media may be said, in normative use, to embody expressive activity and to embody it by means of some materialization that may include word, image, action, reproduction, representation, or whatever. I exclude from my notion of media the ordinary though somewhat strange usage of an art form as a medium. Someone who performs a dance is performing and expressing; the dance is the expression, and thus I do not consider the dance to be a "medium." Instead, a medium is necessarily something between the expressor of the expressive activity and the recipient, just as the spiritualist medium is presumably "between" the living and the dead. By being situated between the direct expressive activity and the recipient, a medium inherently occupies a potentially hermeneutic role. (The hermeneut is an interpreter, for example, the priest or oracle who conveys the messages of the gods.)

By so defining the media-situation—a definition I think will be seen to be appropriate to the phenomenon—I also may relate media to the phenomenological understanding of intentionality. The nonmediated situation may be symbolized as follows:

$$\text{Human} \rightleftarrows \text{World}$$

In this symbolization the intentional interaction with the world may be described as direct. I have in mind what I earlier called face-to-face situations. Here normal human dialogue may be taken as the paradigm. When you and I speak face to face our mutual experience is directed toward each other. The perceptual situation is such that the full play of the senses is open—I see your gestures, hear your intonations, feel your expressive presence, and so forth. Such a situation is unmediated. Thus in such situations I shall not speak of media.

If, however, I were to speak to you over a telephone, the situation is dramatically altered. In this case, the dialogue is not face to face, but mediated by means of the telephone. The telephone as a medium is between us. This may be symbolized with respect to intentionality:

Human——————— medium——————→ World
(I——————— telephone——————→ You)

This formalism takes account of a medium in mediating position. The artifact (telephone) is taken into intentionality and occupies a mediating position.

First, note that the medium of the telephone is such that it may be said to embody the dialogue; it makes your voice present to me and mine to you. In so doing, the artifact, when functioning well, "withdraws" or becomes semitransparent as noted. At optimum function, I am able to recognize your voice as yours, and although your presence to me is reduced perceptually to a mere voice, the presence is one in "real space-time." This capacity of a medium to materialize us to each other in spite of vast geographical distances is, of course, one of the advantages of media. I call this advantage the *amplificatory dimension* of media. A medium makes something possible either in a sense of enhancing an ordinary possibility—for example, the megaphone enhances the volume of the voice so that it carries farther and louder than ordinarily—or in a more radical sense of providing the condition of possibility for something not before possible—the transatlantic telephone carries the voice to distances simply not possible in any face-to-face situation. But the advantage is gained at a price. Your presence to me through the telephone is—compared to global perception—a reduced presence and lacking in the perceptual richness of the face-to-face situation.

I call this the *reductive dimension* of a medium. Simultaneous with and inextricably bound to the amplificatory dimension (which is usually regarded positively) is the reductive dimension, which subtracts something from the richness of ordinary, global experience. I am here illustrating this structural characteristic of media by what happens perceptually.

Together, this amplification-reduction makes a medium nonneutral or transformative of human experience. It is, moreover, a feature of every use of a technology. The term "nonneutrality" is carefully chosen so as to preclude either some immediate "good" or equally immediate "bad" connotation for technologies. It is, rather, essentially or invariably ambiguous, and this inescapable ambiguity makes the use and development of technologies simultaneously fascinating, threatening, and in need of serious reflection.

Not only does a technology contain in its use an invariantly transformational factor, but it does so in a specific way. Every technology has what I call a *telos*, or weighted center of gravity that makes it partially selective as to what may be enhanced and what reduced.

In the example of the telephone, if all I need is information, the telephone seems relatively adequate; but if you are my wife or other intimate, although the immediacy of the telephone is better than the more "abstract" letter, there remains a sense of lack. (Here imaginative compensations may occur to fill in the experience, but in contrast to the possibility of genuine face-to-face contact these remain only a partial satisfaction.) Here we begin to sense what might be called a center of gravity to a given medium, a center that is only relatively adequate to some purposes and less so to others.

And even if the telephone permits genuine embodiment of a real space-time dialogue, it does not do so without transforming that dialogue. The space-time of a telephone conversation has a certain irreal character to it as well. For example, the space-time of such a conversation is always that of a near distance. This distance is neither geographical, in the sense of having a clear perception of far and near, nor the distance of normal lifespace as in dialogue space. It is rather the mediated space-time in which all distances are made quasi-near (I can hear you just about as well from the next town as from California or even Europe—if the technology is good), but equivalently you are never perceptually fully present and thus you remain simultaneously irreally distant. In short, the medium transforms the other and the situation in which the other is made present. This transformation is non-neutral.

So far, I have taken a familiar situation and begun to unravel its effects within what are for us normal experiences. Familiarity often covers over what may be noted to be quite striking effects. We do not think twice about telephones, yet they dramatically transform the possibility of human dialogue, making it possible in situations never before available, but also making it possible by transforming the very meaning of the presence and location of the other.

The telephone is a monosensed medium and thus is a partial sensory experience. This partiality is, moreover, ambiguous. Its familiar mediation is such that we now have habitual patterns of telephone relations that we take for granted. There is currently much experimentation with an audiovisual form of communication, a television-phone. The ambiguity of our habit is pointed up by the mixed response to such a device—some think it would be nice to be able to see the other as well as talk to him or her, while others, on second thought, note that they might well be caught with hair in curlers or without their pajamas. There are both advantages and disadvantages to the partiality. The telephone as a medium has been taken into daily life in a certain way. And we organize our communication patterns around the peculiar capacities of instrumental embodiment. Such effects are subtle, and because they are so familiar, we may fail to take note of the way our experience of the other has been transformed.

A more complex medium—let us take television—displays the same essential features. Although the television is bisensory (audiovisual), it remains both an extension of our sensory experience in space-time and a reduction of that experience. In this instance the transformation of space-time may be quite dramatic, so much so that the "live" performance is the exception to the general practice of replay in which the immediate lifeworld reference may no longer even exist. I only too well recall the somewhat ghoulish anticigarette commercial in which a recently dead actor had pretaped his moral not to smoke. He indicated that he would be dead of lung cancer when seen on television. The television brings what was past and what is or was elsewhere into the near-distance of the media *now*. In this sense it reinforces our experience of an irreal presence of mediated otherness. The quasi-abstract character of the television image remains untouchable and distant while simultaneously being present here and now. But what stands forth as the focal phenomenon is the pervasive presence of the mediated now, the near-distance of what is heard and viewed.

The extension-reduction of media has another facet as well. In format, contemporary television (at least in capitalist countries) differentiates little between the seven o'clock news and Walt Disney. A report on deaths in a world revolution could just as well be interrupted by a commercial as could segments of a cartoon feature. But the point here is not a diatribe against commercialism; it is rather the observation that space-time in the medium takes on a certain disjunctive character. The medium has as a capacity, a technological "transcendence," over ordinary space-time. The freedom of control possible in editing and constructing a program is closer to the reverie, to the imaginative dimension, than to ordinary life. (This is obviously not to extoll the current "imaginativeness" of television!) It has, therefore, the same tempting power as the more ancient medium, print, for those who wish to escape from tedium, boredom, and the ordinary. The viewer may escape into the reproduced reverie just as the reader of pulp novels may do.

I do not intend, in this characterization, to suggest that escape is the only possibility of media such as print or television—to the contrary, the extension that is possible to a wider world of humanity, nature, or whatever is also a possibility. I am suggesting, however, that the extension is of a particular kind, that it simultaneously reduces, amplifies, and transforms the referent to some particular mediated response.

The media world is thus a transformed world. I am not saying that it is either merely an imitation of or reproduction of the ordinary perceptual world. But I am saying that it is a variant "world." So far, the level of analysis has varied only between direct perceptual situations in which no media are positioned and mediated perceptual situations in which media occupy some position between the experiencer and the referent of the experience. However, a complication enters this situation. The mediated perceptual situation remains in a basic sense perceptual. It is I who see the television; I who hear the voices. And while the presumed ultimate referent is somewhere else, I also immediately perceive the television presence. This is to make the obvious point that all experience has its perceptually basic dimension, but it is also to point to something else. Insofar as the medium is immediately experienced, it also transforms the larger perceptual situation. Indeed, media become part of the total perceptual situation. And if at the first level one may detect the irreal dimension of a mediated perception, at a second level one can also claim that this mediation has now been materialized and thus becomes part of reality. This is, of course, to say that media have a "real" effect.

At this level the real effect of media has certain implications for the way we interpret our overall experience. I shall describe this effect by a series of gradations such that initial analogies that are taken to be metaphorical gradually become the common coin and are taken to be literal. For example, in much psychological description and certainly in that which records descriptions of experience by subjects, it is now common to describe imagination, memory, dreams, and other image-related experience as "like" a movie. At this stage we have a clear example of cross-sorting in which there are obvious analogies between two distinctly different phenomena. What tends to get emphasized are, in fact, the similarities rather than the differences although the differences may well be as important as the similarities.

Such cross-sorting has often become so traditional that it becomes assumed that the likeness is virtually identical. In epistemology one may illustrate this by referring to the long and deeply held traditions that claim that imagination reproduces perception and is isomorphic with it, whereas this is simply phenomenologically false. (For example, the focal plane of visual imagination is quite distinct from that of perception in that it is "shallower." Furthermore, the relation and ratio of the core reference imaginatively is and can be radically different than in perception. In the imagined Pegasus, the field within which it is located imaginatively can be so vague and indistinct as to mislead the imaginer into thinking there is no ground for the figure at all, whereas perceptually one can attempt to ignore the background, but once pointed out it becomes obvious that there is no painted Pegasus except against a ground.[4])

In the first cross-sorting approximation, the similarities are merely noted and distinctions glossed over. Life becomes "like" the movies just as movies may be lifelike. (Many persons remark that it seems as if they have "seen this movie before" or report that they feel as though they have "been in this movie before.")

Note that in this cross-sorting, causal relations or relations of origination may work in either direction. Certainly prior to the experience of movies and television, imagination and memory would not have been described as "movielike." Rather, imaginers and rememberers inverted the process and often deliberately modeled their sequences upon imaginations and memories (as did literature before). But once having become part of the lifeworld, the dream-imagined-remembered sequences now materialized become part of the way we come to understand ourselves and our world.

At the other end of the process of cross-sorting in which a metaphorical relation becomes understood as nonmetaphorical, one can also discern a relation to media-induced experience. In recent years I have attended a number of interdisciplinary conferences dealing with computer technology and artificial intelligence. To my constant amazement I find that there are always a number of participants (usually mathematicians and highly theorectially oriented computer programmers) who take the human mind and the computer not to be metaphorically similar, but (potentially) literally identical. Here the process of cross-sorting has lost its suggestive analogical basis and has become a metaphysics.[5] But this phenomenon should be expected by a phenomenologist. If it is the case that intentionality is genuinely interactive between world and self, and if that "world" increasingly becomes encapsulated or at least focused upon some narrow set of intriguing phenomena, then at least for the noncritical and reductively predisposed mind it becomes almost inevitable that "I" will become "like" my experienced "world."

I am suggesting that a technological world is not only one in which we are increasingly related to the media, but that such relations are nonneutral in at least two important senses. I have shown how the transformation of basic perceptual experience occurs in the experience of media, and now I have suggested that at the level of human self-interpretation the experience of media becomes pervasive and familiar and begins to inform our ways of understanding ourselves. I suggest that this effect is pervasive and subtle (and it is not linear in that single items or developments would be hard, if not impossible, to detect), but it is an effect that is hard to demonstrate globally.

A global effect can probably only be hinted at speculatively. I shall conclude this foray into media by suggesting one such possible global effect. At the more microanalytic level of a phenomenological analysis of the telephone, I suggested that the medium of the telephone transformed our usual perceptual sense of space-time into what I termed an irreal near-distance. I would contend that this feature is in fact invariant in experienced media and is enhanced by the more complex media such as film or television. But as we experience such media not only more frequently but also more dominantly, we gradually become so familiar and habituated to this way of relating to the world that its initially sharp variation with the nonmedia world becomes less distinct. This, in turn, allows the condition of the possibility of transformed space-time to be increasingly taken as "real" space-time.

What would such a space-time be? In part, the answer is approximately a near-distant space-time in which all "spaces" and "times" are made quasi-near. That this is a media capacity is clear. Kennedy's assassination, Vietnam, even the news hour replays of old newsreels, complemented by the fictional futuresque movies of *Star Wars* and the like, bring such "spaces" and "times" into the now. But, although media space-time has the possibility of making near, it does so always at a distance, a distance that reduces the perceptual or fully lived sense of the phenomenon. The media-phenomenon is hermeneutic—it is mediated. Its presence is a distant presence that needs the adumbration of critical imagination to "come alive."

Once again the analogy to that now ancient medium, print, emerges. The new media have capacities which writing has always had—but with a difference. Precisely as the medium approximates perceptual experience (the cinema brings the action before one, one does not have to imagine it), it becomes ever more difficult to be a mere observer. Instead, the near-distant space-time of media has as a center of gravity, on the part of the viewer, a viewing that is something like an "aesthetic stance."

An aesthetic stance in this speculation is a stance between what could be called "observer consciousness" and direct actional involvement. Again a series of graded examples can show the weighted form of viewing which is implied. A viewing that is primarily that of observer consciousness is detached, the kind of viewing we ordinarily associate with the highly perceptive but personally distinct viewing of an experiment. Such a viewing, to be sure, implies a discipline to be constituted and implies a subterranean commitment to certain ideals such as those entailed in scientific enterprises. At the other end of the continuum would be direct actional involvement such as we find in the normal affairs of daily life. With friends, family, and colleagues our engagements are primarily actional. But with the speculative aesthetic stance implied in the media experience, we find both a distance and an involvement of a peculiar sort. Cinema and television do not call for immediate action—the bumpkin who jumps on the stage to slug the villain in a melodrama would be the counterexample to an appropriate distance in media viewing. But neither does the expressive activity presented through media leave us without engagement. It engages the wider spectrum of our experience, including our emotional life, but it engages it in the near-distance of a dramalike situation.

Once again this analysis of contemporary media calls forth reflections of long familiar experience, the experience of reading and literature and the experience of the performing arts, each of which entices a variation of an aesthetic stance for our response. But what is different in the contemporary use of media is not only the extent of media use, which virtually permeates much contemporary life, but the same enticement toward aesthetic stance in daily life. Cinema and television are still primarily entertainment devices or information devices that can be seen to be most clearly use situations appropriate for the aesthetic stance. But telephones, the increasing use of other communications media, and even the communications uses of television-mediated interpersonal engagements bring this stance into the vicinity of action.

The larger and even more speculative question that arises from this observation can be hinted at both by way of an open conclusion and a suggestive question: Does the daily experience of media incline though not determine our experience of others increasingly toward a shaped world that reflects the essential possibilities of media? To put it crudely, does the near-distance essential to the experience of media, does the possibility of the disjunction in space-time, does the very concept of "role" now analogous to dramatic play, incline us toward a particular form of social life? Were we to observe that contemporary life reflected this pattern in terms of human relations in which roles are significantly and frequently shifted, in which any person potentially could be a "relationship," in which discontinuities were taken to be as normal as continuities, we might have food for thought regarding the more global impact of media upon our form of life.

Looking into the Media:
Revelation and Subversion

John O'Neill

It is so difficult to think about the media that after some reflection we are likely to conclude that our difficulty derives from the fact that the media thinks itself or, rather, that what is not thought and felt and said through the mass media—if not through the elite media of literature and the arts—is not worth thinking, feeling, or saying. This impasse reproduces our general passivity before television, newspapers, advertisements, films, and sporting spectacles. One is either a player, a committed commentator, or a fan—but hardly ever is a place kept for the contemplative mind. Not to know what is going on in the media is to be out of it. To claim to know more than what is going on in the media than the media allow for, however, is to be out of joint with the form and content of the media. Critics of the media are exiles, or else they are allowed to strut their brief moment among life's killjoys, as a reminder of those higher things for which we have neither the time nor the taste. TV or not TV, that is the question!

Critics, or plain interpreters of the media, must decide to be or not to be. Failing silence, they must gather their own act, acquire a self, and imagine a society within which to think, to feel, and to speak otherwise—for awhile at least. I shall try in this essay to think together an otherwise infinite variety of media models, scenes, sporting and meteorological events, along with the seemingly commercial values that are delivered daily into our homes without any of us quite knowing how we came to live within such an avalanche of images. Our concern, then, is with how the media of newsprint, film,

music, and television convey to us life itself and not simply
how to live, how to eat, how to dress, how to love or to suffer,
how to injure or to kill. Our task is to interpret how these
media convey to us a life that is no longer an alternative life,
or an amusement, or a fiction. For to suppose that the media
are merely adjuncts to our living is to suppose that the family,
the school, the church, and the university are central to our
living. It is to suppose that adults know who they are and that
they know what they want; it is to suppose that parents know
more than children; it is to believe that men and women
understand the difference between social relations and sexual
relations, the difference between love and cruelty, between
commitment and contract. It is to suppose that we understand
the difference between the state and society, between the
home and the economy, between education and entertainment. It is to believe that men and women can tell the days
apart and that they still hope for some difference between
today and tomorrow, not because they wish to leave today
behind, but because they wish it to be remembered with the
rest of the past.

It is the daily business of the media to confirm these beliefs
while destroying them. Thus our follies are never beneath
reason and our reason is never more than a limited folly.
Therein lies the field of phenomenological criticism, which
accepts the convivial limits of reason while nevertheless
claiming to be authentic. Such criticism has its counterpart in
the celebration of everyday life begun by Montaigne, Proust,
and Joyce, for example, inasmuch as the literary redemption
of the profundity of ordinary living can be achieved only
through sounding dreams and myth.[1] In other words, I have
in mind in the following arguments a concern for critical
understanding that does not exploit the differences between
the way things are and the way they might be. Rather, I wish
to leave open the possibility of their reversal through our care
of what is sublime as well as what is desperate in our affairs
and the times we are living through.

To make any beginning in thinking the media, we need to consider technology as revelation, to regard our machines as the prime instruments of appearances, of dreams, of visions, and of truth in the assertions of skyscrapers, cathedrals, banks, theaters, automobiles, television, newsprint, rock music, refrigerators, and contraceptives that furnish everyday life with its average sense and nonsense. Therefore, it is ourselves we see in television and in print commercials because we express ourselves in these media only with greater exaggeration than in the rest of our living. To show what I have in mind, I propose to interpret several communicative artifacts—a paper mat, a potpourri of commercials, and some misreadings of rock, open theater, and urban graffiti. I shall try to find in these varied communicative media how it is we reveal and subvert the deepest, the most trivial, the most holy, and the most vulgar of our beliefs and values.

If Woodstock, as Abbie Hoffman has remarked, was an attempt to land man on earth, then that even larger celebration of America's birthday must be viewed as a more determined effort to land man right in America. We shall return to Woodstock. But let us begin with the Bicentennial as a communicative artifact in which the commonest things express to Americans who they are in what they eat and, fundamentally, in how they choose to eat.

The Media of Our Discontents

The Declaration of Independence provided Americans with a machinery of *divine discontent* without which we cannot understand American political economy:

> We hold these truths to be self-evident: that all men are created equal; that they are endowed by their creator with certain inalienable rights; that among these are life, liberty, and the pursuit of happiness; that to secure these rights, governments are instituted among men, deriving their just powers from the

consent of the governed; that whenever any form of government becomes destructive of these ends, it is the right of the
people to alter or to abolish it.[2]

I shall argue that America is built upon a communicative
machine known as the American Way of Life. This machinery
operates a process of *commodification,* which materializes the
ideals in the Declaration of Independence in an endless flow
of deals in the marketplace. Because of the massive rhetoric of
the American Way of Life, there is no place for any other
revolution than the first American Revolution. The result is
that whereas in Europe everyone is revolutionary but few are
subversive, in America no one is revolutionary, though many
are subversive. This was first observed by Alexis de Tocqueville, and I believe his observations are as good today as they
were over a hundred years ago:

> I have often remarked, that theories which are of a revolution-
> ary nature, since they cannot be put into practice without a
> complete and sometimes a sudden change in the state of prop-
> erty and persons, are much less favorably viewed in the
> United States than in the great monarchial countries of Eu-
> rope; if some men profess them, the bulk of the people reject
> them with instinctive abhorrence. I do not hesitate to say that
> most of the maxims commonly called democratic in France
> would be proscribed by the democracy of the United States.
> This may easily be understood: *in America men have the opin-
> ions and passions of democracy; in Europe we have still the
> passions and opinions of revolution.*[3]

The truth of Tocqueville's remarks has been marvelously
absorbed by the commercial media of the American corporate
economy. I can only begin to explore this phenomenon. Consider Exhibit I *(A Declaration).* It is a paper place mat from a
large chain restaurant, Howard Johnson's, a landmark all over
America, famous for its twenty-eight varieties of ice cream.
Howard Johnson's is a sign among all the other road signs that

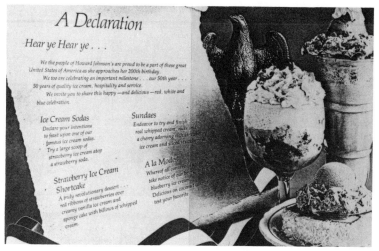

Exhibit I *(A Declaration)*

show Americans where to gas up, feed, amuse, sleep, and toilet as they move along highways whose only respite from the speeds they afford is the signposts that offer to just as speedily service the weary traveler in order to return him to the highway. Howard Johnson's is a traveler's icon, the same everywhere he goes, offering the same variety of food in the same restaurant, welcoming the traveler free to roam in one of the world's most orderly traffic flows. America's Bicentennial celebration was not at all desecrated by Howard Johnson's use of the Declaration of Independence. On the contrary, the desecration of the American creed—its commodification—is essential to the daily practice of American democracy. As long as the rights to life, liberty, and the pursuit of happiness can be translated into the commodifications of ice cream, automobiles, travel, and smoking, enjoyed by a public willing to consume the shoddy look-alikes of mass production in their homes, clothing, amusement, and education, the American dream is given an individual fit. It makes itself something that people can grasp in a tangible form. At the same time, everything Americans do grasp must also reflect their aspirations to higher things enjoyed in this world.

Ice cream is a perfect example of the artifactuality of the American dream. Ice cream is a hybrid of nature and industry. It fulfills a desire that by themselves neither nature nor industry—or even our own mother—could satisfy, except for the know-how that brings them all together. It is a gift that recruits children forever into a world of endless variety from whose cares it will later free them along with all the other self-rewarding foods and drinks that make up popular eating habits. Ice cream, if not the ice cube, is the totemic food of Americans. It accomplishes the infantilization and permanent communion of Americans in the variety of choice and the happiness of a food that symbolizes the unity of nature and industry produced playfully as a bounty of the promised land. Americans easily identify their rights to life, liberty, and the pursuit of happiness with their quest for wholesome food available in endless variety and at very little cost. It is central to the American way of life that the quest for food not symbolize human suffering and exploitation. It is this that distinguishes them from foreigners and natives and thereby motivates American charity.

Consider Exhibit II *(The American Way with Food)*. The text is remarkable for the ease with which it makes the choices of religion, occupation, and government resemble the choices consumers make in a supermarket. The identification of food choices with religious, economic, and political freedom in turn overdetermines the belief that the latter institutions are in a gross way the outcome of the same individual choice and caprice that go into buying cakes and cookies. The powers of church, state, and economy are denied any determining influence upon the sovereign consumer. Thus the harsh realities that govern the everyday obligations of law, labor, and belief

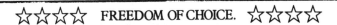

☆☆☆☆ FREEDOM OF CHOICE. ☆☆☆☆

There are three words so uniquely American that they can describe a whole way of life—but so familiar that their meaning can be easily overlooked:

Freedom of Choice.

Freedom to choose an occupation. A religion. A government. To make of your life what you will, not what you are ordered.

We invite you to give fresh consideration to those words, not as some grand ideal but rather as they describe the life you live every day. For in that way, the celebration of the American birthday takes on a huge importance.

Freedom of choice—every day. Nowhere in the American economy will you find a better example than in the very food you eat. Walk into a supermarket and you'll find literally thousands of choices—choices that let you, and you alone, determine exactly what and how you want to eat.

That's the American way with food, and that's what The Pillsbury Company is all about. For

baking from scratch, generations of Americans have depended on Pillsbury's Best* Flour. But, suppose you want to make a cake off with a ready-made frosting. Pillsbury, at your service. Or how about refrigerated biscuits you bake and serve, or dinner rolls, or hearty pancakes—the choices go on and on.

The American way with food is *your* way. And we're proud that so many of the products that let you make your own choices come from The Pillsbury Company.

Exhibit II *(The American Way with Food)*

are removed from consciousness in favor of a down-to-earth interpretation of the ideal of freedom as the American way with food. In exchange for his ignorance of the underlying realities of the American political economy, the consumer is made wise, pragmatic, and omnipotent in the exercise of trivial choices of breakfast and snack foods. The products themselves are made to appeal via the tropes of family, tradition, fun, health, and the rights of children. They make ordinary things and occasions into special and extraordinary experiences. They are made by a large corporation with a homey face, dedicated to the family and the kids, relieving mother from baking while instilling in her the feeling that she might have baked all the good things on the Pillsbury table.

The commodification of the American Revolution collapses the historical awareness of Americans, while at the same time reviving it in the commercial sagas of the wild West, antique hunting, and the retailing of the American heritage in volumes that decorate coffee tables or provide ammunition for the tireless projects of competitive schoolchildren. If the past is to survive, it must contribute to the future by seeming to be either an irresistible impulse to national progress or a collection of handy facts for children on the make in school. Thus, in the popular mind American history owes far more to the movies than to the poor competition of its school book versions. In the first place, there was the promised land of the early settlers. Admittedly, the land had to be cleared of Indians. But even this work was democratized by the six-shooter and the rifle. Later, the tractor cleared the white farm families themselves from the land, as corporate and industrialized agriculture began to feed the cities and the factories of America. If there was a victim in the wars against the Indians or in the Civil War (it took the Vietnam War to give the blacks their roots in white America) it was the farmer, whom America today, forgetful of the grapes of wrath remembers only as a six-shooting cowboy—or as Bonnie and Clyde, shooting at a world of corporate finance and controls they cannot grasp. Indeed, the cowboy and the gangster—the poor boys of town and countryside—hold the American imagination precisely because they are innocent of the ways of corporate organization, yet are devoted to the same ideals of success—a big spread, a huge ranch, a big car, and a big cigar—that are packaged in less heroic and more routine fashion for the corporate worker and consumer.

If the huge fortunes and the corporate organization of country and western music[4] do not disturb the downtrodden and divinely rehabilitated images of its heroes, it is because country and western music audiences are the loyalist branch of the American dream. In the same vein, the recent success of the Mafia-inspired *Godfather* films is intelligible if we understand that they restore successful violence to the American family, reviving ethnic loyalty as the enemy of anonymously rational corporate organization. The formal similarity remains even in *Dog Day Afternoon*, which joyfully celebrated the bungling criminality of an Italian, Catholic homosexual at grips with the organized overkill of the police. The movies are an American artifact. They are as necessary to the communication of American political life as the hot dog, the automobile, cowboys and Indians, and cops and robbers are elemental to the community they portray. The movies are a continuous American mass, celebrating the great theme of individualized success and failure that is also the daily bread of the American cartoon strip.[5] The movies are the depoliticized revelation of the American Revolution. However momentarily, they recruit everyone into the popcorn lumpen-proletariat that dreams of a sudden reevaluation of its original rights to participation in the American dream. The American passion for documenting failure, for celebrating the underdog as much as it celebrates success in business, sports, crime, and beauty contests, is a passion for documenting the Declaration of Independence. Moreover, it is a passion that makes politics fun—it allows the business of keeping an eye on the American charter to be carried on as an amusement activity, the pastime of paid-up members consuming the offerings of legitimate theater or journalism. For these reasons, the newspaper and the movies are perfectly integrated communicative mechanisms of de-politicized conscientiousness, inasmuch as they are consumed in private, familized settings, in free time, and thus removed from the political motivations of a real public.[6] The spectator who contemplates the saga of success and failure learns from failure that success is better. "Success," of course, is not the sheer matter of winning; it is the practice of freedom and abundance on individual terms. It is a practice that requires a world of opposition that contains only other individuals or the sheer otherness of nature (including primitives and colonials) red in tooth and claw. Thus the myth of success and failure is a depoliticized myth—the Revolution as a Way of Life—that hides the stratifying realities of class, racism, and corporate power that otherwise shape the American's exercise of his/her rights to life, liberty, and the pursuit of happiness.

Commercial Bodies

Marx argued that all production is social. I want to include in the notion of production, not just the body's physical labor, but every experience, sensation, and activity of the body as a field of production and consumption. By this I mean that we must regard the *productive body*[7] as an extension of the econ-omy and not simply as a factor of production, like labor. Like labor power, the productive body exists only in a market economy, which is capable of reifying its stress, relaxation, health, illness, beauty, spontaneity, and sexuality. The reification of the body within industrial and commercial sec-tors concerned with its production and consumption inte-grates and distributes the body throughout the economy. The productive body is not a factor of production in the way that Marx envisaged land, labor, and capital. The productive body is integrated into the division of labor, both internally, as through modern medicine, and externally, as through fashion and cosmetics. Thus the productive body is both an extension and an intensification of the space and activity of the modern economy. It is not simply that the economy expropriates the labor of the body, subjecting it to pain in its tasks and to an unsatisfactory standard of living in return for its wages. The most massive exploitation of the body occurs as the economy teaches us to disvalue our body in its natural state and only to revalue our body once it has been sold grace, spontaneity, vivaciousness, bounce, confidence, smoothness, and fresh-ness. The media are a principal socializing agency in those techniques of the body[8] that display the cultural values of youth, aggression, mobility, and sociability. By the same token, the media are obliged to hide the ordinary condition of men, women, and children, except as a shock or removed misery. In all this, television unites the family the better to divide it. The more the modern family unit is geared to con-sumption, the more it needs to separate into wage earners who separate sexuality and reproduction. Thus the female body must be deromanticized and made the instrument only of rational, that is, contractual associations. Trusting to the pill, young women's bodies are made mobile for work, high-rise living, and adventure. The physical hazards, ranging from cancer to rape, are all part of this bodily complex that sings its appeal to the young self-possessed women of the cigarette and perfume world.

We shall not understand the spectacular functions of the communications industry unless we think of the hold it has upon us as literally a grip upon our bodies, turning the body into a theater of corporeal agony and ecstasy. We must realize what the media realize, namely, that the body is the theater of all our desires, of our salvation and destruction, of beauty and ugliness, of joy and pain. The body is the seat of science and of religion, of psychoanalysis and politics. It is above all an endless topic and resource for the communicative media:

> The body, like the body politic, is a theatre; everything is symbolic, everything including the sexual act. The principal part is a public person taking the part of the community as a whole: *persona publica totius communitatis gerens vicem*. The function of the representative organ is to impersonate, incarnate, incorporate in his own body the body politic. Incorporation is the establishment of a theatre (public); the body of spectators depend on the performance for their existence as one body.[9]

The body is the theater of our social life. It projects the spectacle of our self-presentations to others as we would wish to be seen by them, as well as being the mirror in which we seek our most private self. The human body is the holy place of expression and concealment; it is the instrument of our transcendence and togetherness, as well as the seat of our withdrawal and sorrow. Our body is our circumstance and our fortune; it is given to us by others, and yet, like nothing else, it is our own. Our body is the seat of our most persistent needs, weighted by the legacy of our ancestors, and yet lightly at the whim of our most fleeting desires, courting the stillborn future of fashion and obsolescence. For the most part we encounter the body when it is too late—overweight, in love, pregnant, or with a broken leg. We experience our body as something uncanny, something suddenly reversible—the cynosure of eyes, sweeping down a staircase to be met by admirers, the source of our shame and embarrassment, should we trip and fall, more like an apple than a star.

As we have learned from countless commercials, the spectacle of the body occupies much of our daily efforts. Beginning with the call to rise and shine, we proceed to wash, polish, scrape, and spray until we are satisfied that we are cheerful-looking, businesslike, alluring, handsome, and even sexy for the next twenty-four hours. Each of us can fantasize his or her own approach to these body rituals. We become Roman empresses when sunk in a bubble bath; or for women who find this too decadent, there is the virgin's struggle with pimples, stringy hair, mouth and body odors, all of which have to be overcome in the half hour before the arrival of the knight in shining armor, Wilkinson's sword, and high karate. For older men, there is the massage parlor, provided it is open to the rush of unmannerly children berserk with their latest cavity count. For the dirty Irish, Erin now grows green soap! The commercials have also taught us what as mechanical and urban men we need to know of nature. It is usual now to speak of the most recent stage of industrial society as one with special features—summarized in the experience of private affluence and public squalor.[10] No contrast is better suited to commercial scenarios. Affluent society is by and large an in-door society. We spend our time inside factories, offices, clubs, automobiles, and houses. These interiors are also machine settings in which most of what we do is done for us. The machines have the power and we have the flab. Precisely because affluent society is an indoor society, we observe a massive exodus from its great dormitories to the countryside, lakes, beaches, and mountains. City dwellers are sports and nature lovers, as well as hi-fi bugs, bookworms, and moviegoers. How are we to understand this? A bewildering variety of vocabularies motivate the quest for nature, sport, and leisure, ranging from positivism and romanticism to militarism and existentialism. People find God and country in the great forests, in the surf, and on snowmobiles. They also find in nature a larger arena for the national pastime of littering, which has its great celebration in the forest fire. Other favorite activities in the great outdoors include the pollution of rivers and lakes with the noise of motor boats, as well as other forms of human dirt. The great outdoors is classically a man's

world, or at any rate it belongs to our John Waynes as well as
to our Tom Sawyers. It is a white man's world, though Ne-
groes and Indians may tag along or serve as bait. Bears, golf-
balls, and fish serve as pretexts for men to go off together for
days on end, under the sponsorship of their favorite brewery,
to celebrate the great male bond to which the human race
owes its survival. Women, though better left at home or
parked in the country clubs, function best in the outdoors as
cooks or as symbols of the renewal of the human race. But
they do not make friends; this is a man's business. Friendship
is found in fieldhouses, locker rooms, sweat and sneakers,
pinches and pats with the boys. "Friendship is the clean-cut,
competitive horsing around of regular guys, for Christ's sake!"
Girls and wives can never understand this, and so it is better
for them to visit mother, or go shopping, take evening
courses, and leave the boys to their night out. In this way, we
learn much of the rhetoric of our daily morality, and not only
of our vice and violence.

We should not overlook that the media have more serious
concerns. Today, more than ever, the tragic spectacle of the
body thrusts itself upon us in the media reports on the victims
of war and civil violence, in the images of helpless victims of
famine and other disasters. It is above all in the agonies of
sport that the human body provides us with a morality play
suited to the rise and fall of industrial man. In the early industrial period, the body spectacles commonly associated
with sport and leisure were the privilege of the surviving
landed aristocracy and the new middle classes. What could be
learned on the playing fields of Eton may hardly have seemed
civilized to the French, but it proved itself on the battlefields
of India, for all its failures in the bedrooms of London and
Paris. The gradual extension of sports to the lower classes, by
and large such lower-class sports as football and visits to the
public baths, depended upon the introduction of the five-and-
a-half-day working week—the remaining half day being given

to Saturday football, beer, and dancing, with the Puritan pro-
vision of the whole Sunday for repentance. Today, commer-
cially punctuated sports spectacles compete with the private
agonies of sex and drugs scored upon the body. For technological man, the places of victory and defeat are by and large
unspectacular—witness the failure of the greatest show on
earth once the Cape Kennedy stagings became regular pro-
ductions. By contrast, modern professional sports, and I
would include here the Hollywood musical and local strip
joint, have become the secular rites of industrial society.

Sports spectaculars are games of position and points, in
which violence and efficiency are sublimated into a statistical
code of victory and defeat, which in turn animates a largely
passive audience. Sports statistics are the history, law, and
science of the average man—the proof that he does not live by
hot dogs and popcorn alone. Modern games are the soul of
objectivity: they culminate in the passionless play of the moon
game and the armaments race. Games, then, are the highest
moments in the media world; they are indistinguishably communication, consummation, and consecration. Sports spectaculars are essentially ritual performances because the very
nature of the escape they involve commits the viewer to the
formal, professional, and technical-legal efficiency involved in
their production. The same is true, I believe, although I shall
not develop the argument here, of the new forms of sexual
play and pornography. In all these activities, the body strives
to become the machine that threatens to replace it in everyday life. In endless replays of the aggressive and competitive
game of industrial society, sports spectaculars encourage the
fantasy that the virtues and vices of industrial society can be
mastered as character and guts.

If outdoor sports have any serious rival, it is from the indoor
sport of weather watching. Nothing is better suited to people
who spend their days moving from one container to another—
from house, to car, to bus, to office, to bus, to car, to house—

than wondering what it feels like in between. The less we experience the weather the more we are concerned with it. It is the perfect obsession. When most people lived on farms they could tell the weather for themselves and with as much predictability as can today's meteorologists. Indeed, prior to television weather forecasts, even urban people could tell the weather. As it is, the weather man, or weather woman, sits indoors and, with the aid of complex technical equipment, maps out the ups and downs, highs and lows of the atmosphere in a nightly school lesson, repeated for the last time of a hundred times a day. But what is the lesson? Do we still yearn for the outdoors, for the body's rhythmic ties to nature and the cosmos? Or is nature the last obstinate vagary in our lives, the hated and admired vehicle of the uncontrollable and unpredictable? If it is, then we can understand our pleasure in the meteorologist's misfortunes. His failures, like her irrelevance, witness to our ambivalent love of science and technology, to our guilty conspiracy against nature. Having constructed a society in which we have nothing in common, the weather remains the last of all our commonplaces. As such, it is stronger than religion and more enduring than the technologies whereby we struggle to harness its forces.

Toward a Theory of Communicative Subversion

Rather than sharing, Americans have preferred to interpret their revolution to themselves in terms of raising the standard of living[11] for all who can successfully compete in the massive organizations of industry, agriculture, and government that sing of the American Way of Life dispensed through toothpaste, nonreturnable bottles, automobiles, telephones, package tours, credit cards, and political conventions. The engine of the American Revolution has been the large corporation, now nearly global in reach and virtually sovereign in the integration of its investment, production, and consumption strategies. Whenever the soulful corporation appears unequal to the American dream, it can count upon the state administration of antidepressants to "revive the economy" and to get the American people moving forward. Although this economy is endemically unable to absorb the young, the old, and the blacks—all of whom must compete with a highly skilled or programmed technology and its continuous "sophistication"—there has been little determination to alter the American concept of revolution, or to redefine it in terms of a radical change in the political economy of the rights to life, liberty, and the pursuit of happiness.

It is in the city, which we must regard as another of our machines for living, where the commodification of the American Revolution is most clearly articulated and where the sanctions of individualized success and failure are also most harsh. Urban life demands from many citizens a daily countercultural response. It requires a subversive practice of *institutional effacing.*[12] By this, I refer to a civic practice whereby the official and ostensible purposes of institutions, places, objects, and processes are substituted or effaced in favor of the proceedings of those who come to use them day by day or only briefly and, as it were, in flight. Thus, large institutions such as hospitals, airports, and universities, places such as hotel foyers, walls, and sidewalks, and things such as cartons and tin cans are all subject to native use, or *bricolage*, that effaces their ostensible meanings in favor of secondary creations and employments. The subversion of the official and planned uses of institutions, places, and things includes the practices known to them of schoolchildren, auto buffs, bums, welfare hustlers, happenings, and subway graffiti. Effacing is especially an urban art of transforming the iconology of industrial and commercial life to meet the real needs and experience of the city's poor, its aged, and its young people— who so often compete unsuccessfully with such middle-class practices of effacement as the gentrification of inner-city neighborhoods, which import the nostalgia of poverty while expelling the poor.

The urban environment, and in particular the ghetto, is the prime target of effacement. It is saturated with signs that fixate and stereotype ready-made experiences, objects, and encounters that stylize the bodies, dress, and vehicular movements of city people.[13] The aesthetics of the city are a flashboard of the exchange values and the icons of commodification that celebrate the commercial life of its denizens. By the same token, the practical aesthetics of the city are noisy, ugly, and hostile to those who are incompetent with the city's official uses and occasions. Everything that is contradictory and incoherent in the material basis of the political economy is reflected in the neonized iconography of the urban environment, in its wealth and poverty, its comforts and dangers, its crime, its sophistication, and its vulgarity. The city is hard on those who are not making it in the city; it crushes and silences them unless they are able to subvert it by creating their own style and unforeseen ways of holding out, getting by, and hitting back. Thus the city is open to the endless necessary profanations and effacements whereby persons otherwise excluded from its ostensible activities make a place for themselves, cut a figure, and hold out where they would otherwise seem to be submerged. It thereby furnishes a genre of television series, from *Kojak* to *Police Woman*, that serve to spectacularize the drama of law and order as an urban morality play.

It is especially in the ghettos that the superabundance of the media-coded imperatives of consumption and the high life of white affluence turn the environment into a wasteland. The ghetto is ugly because it lacks the decent aesthetics of working-class neighborhoods where work and consumption are closely tied to the rhythm of a steady pay check and the solidarity of labor. The ghetto is simultaneously atomized and

collectivized by the flood of consumption signals fed into it by
television, billboard advertisements, and welfare payments.
It is against this flood of prefabricated meanings that we might
interpret the subversive activity of the New York graffiti
artists.[14] Consider Exhibit III. By expropriating the surfaces

Exhibit III

of walls, elevators, buses, and subway trains, the graffiti have
effaced the semiotic medium of an order, cleanliness, and
commerce from which the ghetto is excluded. Moreover, the
reappropriation of these surfaces is marvelously calculated so
as to be exportable outside the ghetto with the same offensive
and alien quality upon other neighborhoods as the ghetto
experiences. The graffiti artists risked their lives and limbs in
order to cover the subway trains with noms de plume—STAR
III—that rival the facticity of the same world that excludes
their youth, spirit, and imagination. By effacing the hot surfaces of the subway—clean as long as it is covered only with
commercial and financial graffiti—the graffiti artists turned
the subway into cool satellites of the ghetto, whirling around

the city in an endless celebration of deeds known only to the artists. The shock, revulsion, and eventual resignation of the commuters merely registered the same accommodation relied upon by commercial advertising.

The graffiti artists reveal to us our own anonymity, our facticity, our fixation in the urban grid. They tell us that the names and numbers given to us can be thrown back into a mobile comic strip passing before our eyes, to rattle through our brains the reminder that the city is a living tissue and not a subway map. The names are ready-made, like the names of most of us. But as graffiti they force us to ask how they got there and why. In this way, they raise the two permanently subversive questions to which anyone's life is open. The vogue of the graffiti artists has already passed, and this will be considered reason enough by many to dismiss its significance. Like many of the student radicals of the cultural revolution, black and Puerto Rican graffiti artists have also made terms with the establishment. Elsewhere I have tried to make a different sense of these matters.[15] I believe that since the 1960s we have witnessed a variety of attempts in art and street politics to challenge the ruling discourse of the corporate economy and its administrative sciences. I do not see any cataclysmic revolution in these events. But I do believe they reveal an underlying practice of communicative subversion that is a civil resource without which institutional change is incapable of achieving the local fit that is the test of its relative successes and failures.

Walter Ong has argued for a certain parallelism between the sequences of communication processes and the Freudian stages of psychosexual development.[16] There are, of course, huge problems in such comparisons, not to speak of the initial abstraction of such a schema. But what is of value in these constructions is the notion that the human sensorium is a structurally and historically produced producer of its own acoustic, visual, tactile, libidinal, and social environment.[17]

Thus it happens that our machines can alter the ratio between the human senses as well as between society and nature. In what I have called *gay technology*[18] in an attempt to interpret the technological display accompanying rock music, I believe we may discern a variety of social forms that return the industrial and political "machine" to the rhythms of life and the body politic. Along these lines, I think that what we might learn from the music of Woodstock, and its attempt to give birth to a new American nation, is a profound subversion of old-order machine culture, technological decorum, and occupational identity. Thus rock music, its artists, and its audiences dissolve the sterility of technology into the convulsive improvisations of violence, love, care, and community. Rock expresses the joyful embrace of life and technology that is the driving vision of the modern world, as well as its own nightmare. The spectacle of rock reveals the world as desire, the body as environment, caught between order and chaos, invoking community, flirting with self-destruction and infantile disorders. But the conventional technological congregation demands decorum in the presence of machines, engines, typewriters, microphones, and television sets. For this reason rock is especially revolting. Its standards of technological decorum are flirtatious, cajoling, argumentative, burlesque, and destructive.

The contemporary arts, however, do not require us all to trip out at Woodstock or in the cold early morning lineups for every rock concert. The literate and middle-aged, happily, can experience the comfortable shocks of modern theater. Open or experimental theater seeks to alter the fixed perspective of an audience bolted to its seat, numbered, and isolated from one another as well as from the players and their action. The assumption built into the conventional theater "setting" is that catharsis is prepared in the distance between the audience and the play. By contrast, the various forms of contemporary open theater challenge the two-dimensional setting of player and audience relations. They jostle audience and players together, introducing the action of the play from points around the audience, exposing the actors' artifice without benefit of backstage. Visual, acoustic, and tactile values suddenly interconnect and reestablish the visceral community suppressed by conventional theater architecture and staging. The theater becomes a playground of communal energy, of excitement, danger, fatigue, and relief. The audience can no longer be sure of having seen the play unless it has participated, helping one another to spot the action and to join it, to seek engagement rather than escape. Thus modern theater subverts individual isolation by rejecting the cool style of corporate business, team work, and tranquilizers. It invokes a communal body, a renewal of impulse and energy, of music and voice hitherto oppressed with notions of self-control, afraid to make a scene or a spectacle of itself. Of course, these things happen. But from the standpoint of the dominant institutions, they reflect the cravings of the insane, the lawless, and the immature, to be contained in our asylums and official holidays.

In modern society the ratio of self and expressive space is so radically diminished that we experience our bodies as shrunken landscapes. Thus, in our literature the typical setting of the modern self is the underground, the tiny room, the prison, the asylum, and the concentration camp. These are the scenarios of modern sociology and of modern theater. We see the self trapped in primitive settings that force it to account for itself as an object, obsessed with the degrees and forms of distance, bewildered by the fear of others who anticipate the slightest deviation in standards of spontaneity, cleanliness, generosity, and courage. It is no wonder, therefore, that these underlying anxieties furnish the materials of so many of our body commercials, as I have tried to show.

The cultural and communicative forces for depoliticized integration and legitimation which I have described as the commodification of the American Revolution make it difficult to discern any long-term trends in the communicative subversion of the American corporate economy. Meantime, it is clear that the Marxist theory of revolution is inadequate because it continues to locate the impulse to resistance and change in the exploitation of productive labor, whereas it is the generalized code or semiotic[19] of the administrative rationalization of economy, society, and polity that must be identified as the point of attack and subversion. An adequate theory of subversion must, therefore, be a theory of the communicative processes of political economy that now mediate production and consumption, language, sexuality, urbanism, suburbanism, nature, culture, youth, and old age. In short, the theory of communicative subversion is a theory of the political economy of the body. It supersedes the Marxist theory of revolution because it generalizes the semiotic of exchange values to every bodily and mental conduct beyond the simple productive labor required to mobilize commitment to a rationally administered economy. It thereby opens up the field of inquiry begun here.

Wild Sociology

The question of the relation between cultural subversion and political revolution is one that appears to divide us into realists and dreamers. Here, at least, appearances are not deceptive. The options of political theory are indeed orders of character. Cultural subversion is avowedly utopian. It is inventive of character and society. In this, however, it is rejected as inadequate knowledge, evidently innocent of sociology, economics, and politics. What is at stake is the unborn sociology of a society reflexively aware of its notions of order and character. In making this issue plain, cultural subversion toys with the dissolution of professional social science and its expert/lay organization of knowledge. It reveals the distance between sociologists and a sociology aware of itself as work with people. Such a sociology dreams of an end to the hierarchy of knowledge suspended in a genuine collectivity of social work. It is a wild sociology—not in the sense that it is prehistorical sociology—but precisely because, within the very history which wild sociology presupposes, it dares to be utopian. The ignorance that determines professional sociology, on the other hand, is precisely its unhistorical knowledge of the present—modified, to be sure, by its construction of history as the past, but never illuminated by a projection of history as utopia. Whereas establishment sociology is concerned with the administration of existing social order, wild sociology is free to project scenarios of alternative orders. This is what is at issue in the crisis of Western social science and the society that it reflects. It is for these reasons that individual awareness of the quality of everyday life—its objects, language, space, time, and needs—erupts into the meaninglessness of the corporate agenda. The politics of experience represents the insurgency of human values at the low points of everyday life in the urban industrial world: at what Henri Lefebvre calls the "zero point" of social experience, where a kind of irrational asceticism is discernible under the apparent affluence and rationality that dominate our lives, but never so completely as to make countercultural response impossible.[20]

This is not to argue that cultural subversion is the only way of revolution today; however, that is not because there is some intrinsically "political" strategy of revolution. I mean rather to remark upon the poverty of our culture as a resource for revolutionary transformation. This is to weigh its failure, its class bias, its fragmentation and frivolity. It is to feel the nervelessness of a culture that is the property of experts, prostituted and destructive of the very style of life that is the underlying promise of all culture. At the same time, it is to touch at this very zero point of culture its promise of the transfiguration of everyday life, not as a canvas to be wiped clean but as the natural light of man.

The Idea of the University and the Communication of Knowledge in a Technological Age

Calvin O. Schrag

In 1873, John Henry Newman published his classic treatise on education, *The Idea of a University Defined*. This event inaugurated a heightening of consciousness on the part of educators about the nature and mission of those institutions of which they were the appointed custodians. Since that time the traffic of publications on the subject, both in books and articles, has been notably heavy. This, I suggest, is an indication that the inquiry into the idea of the university needs to be taken up time and again. The mission of the university as a social institution and as an educational program is a topic that requires the most durable human resources of critical reflection. This is particularly the case as the university finds itself in a period of history marked by unprecedented social change and technological innovation. It is an urgent demand of the times that we apply the Socratic requirement of self-understanding to the institutional life of the university. The unexamined university is not worth operating.

I shall begin this examination of the idea and mission of the university with a parable. For want of a more poetic title, I call it "The Parable of the Student Who Couldn't Find the University of Alabama."

And in those days, behold, there came to the city of Tuscaloosa a student from afar off. This student came with his loins well-girded with high school math, American and world history, and English literature, wearing the breastplate of advanced chemistry plus a dash of economics and a sprinkling of sociology. And it came to pass that those who made his acquaintance immediately recognized him as a student of singular and uncommon talents, but also as a student with an uncommon and somewhat distressing problem—he couldn't find the University of Alabama!

The problem became apparent his very first day on campus. With all of the excitement and enthusiasm of one embarking on a new venture he asked a befriended senior colleague if he might show him the university. The senior colleague, possessing all of the academically instilled virtues of benevolence, patience, and a long-suffering nature, obliged. He escorted him to the Ferguson Center, the Amelia Gayle Gorgas Library, the Rose Administration Building, the Alumni Hall, the Gorgas Home, the Memorial Coliseum, and so on—to every building on the campus—topping it off with a trek to the President's Mansion; for this senior colleague was indeed intent on doing his job well. Now, at the end of this arduous tour, the senior colleague was exceedingly puzzled when the young student turned to him and said: "Now, this is all very fine—but where is the University of Alabama?"

Not being one to shirk his responsibility, the senior colleague assured the newcomer that he would find some way to show him the university, but after all, getting to know a university takes time, because there are indeed many things to be shown. So during the following days, weeks, and months the senior colleague accepted his charge with an unparalleled singleness of purpose. He introduced his young friend not to tens but to thousands of students. He introduced him to all of the professors that he knew plus many that he did not know. He even presented him to a number of administrators—who happened to be in town for the day. He escorted him to all of the laboratories and displayed to him the intricate workings thereof. He took him on a tour of the physical plant and gave him an opportunity to chat with the custodians and the janitors. He showed him the Tennis Complex, the Baseball Diamond, the Track Field, and then climaxed the odyssey with a visit to the Bryant-Denny Stadium and brought him face to face with Bear Bryant himself.

You can well imagine the consternation and anguish that overcame our senior colleague, when after all this, the young student turned to him and innocently asked, "But where is the University of Alabama?" Our senior colleague was now mightily astonished and utterly dismayed. With the patience of Saint Francis of Assisi, he had shown him the buildings, the laboratories, the students, the professors, the administrators, the coaches—all of which make up the University of Alabama. At least, so he had thought. After all, if the University of Alabama is not the summation of its parts, in whatever fashion these parts are serialized, then what in the name of heaven is it? His patience having expired, our senior colleague now takes his leave, and our weary and bedraggled youthful scholar is left to chance and circumstance.

Now, this chance and circumstance, as either fate or the gods would have it, thrusts him straightway into the back row of a philosophy class in which a lecture on the philosophy of Plato is in progress. As the lecture proceeds, he is struck by the remarkable similarities between Plato's problem concerning the city-state in Athens and his own problem concerning the university in Tuscaloosa. As he follows the lecture, it soon becomes evident to him that he has been asking a wrong-headed question, or, to be somewhat more precise, he has been looking for an answer that is incommensurate with the question that he has been asking. What is at issue, at rock bottom, is not "Where is the University of Alabama?" but "What is the University of Alabama?" And this is very much like Plato's search for an answer to the question, "What is a good city-state?" Or, to put matters a little more directly, what he wants and what he needs so desperately is a grasp of the *idea* or *essence* of the university, of which the complex at Tuscaloosa is hopefully an example; just as Plato was intent on apprehending the universal idea of a city-state of which the newly reconstituted government of Athens would be an instance or exemplification. Hitherto he has confused a "where" question with a "what" question, and this is particularly unfortunate when the question interrogates an idea. Ideas, our young scholar learns from Plato, are not the sorts of things that are locatable in space; indeed, they do not seem to be like things at all. Ideas are invisible realities apprehended not by the physical eye but by the eye of the mind. Plato may not be clear about much, but he does seem to be clear about that.

But if you think that this reformulation of our searching scholar's question, and Plato's alleged answer to it, have ipso facto resolved his predicament, then you have that proverbial second guess coming. No, indeed, it is only now that his problem begins in earnest. As he reflects on the matter, he is reminded of the puzzlement he experienced sometime back in Sunday School, where there was much talk about the difference between the visible and the invisible church—and about all that he gleaned from that was that the invisible church was the church you couldn't see! If he couldn't get things straight about the invisible church, then how will he ever get things straight about the invisible university; and if he can't get things straight about the university, then how can he get things straight about that which exists in Tuscaloosa?

At this juncture, our prolix parable comes to a close—in *media res*, one might say, for our distraught young scholar is left pretty much in the middle of things, puzzling over the idea of a university, which he is unable to grasp. But we hope that we have followed him in his quest far enough for us to achieve some identification with him and to realize that his problem is also ours.

The question as to the idea of the university is assuredly as difficult as it is unavoidable. It is difficult because we appear to be denied any ready access to an abiding essence or meaning, much less a universal image, that attaches to the word "university." The university is a historical institution, and as such it bears the inscriptions of its responses to the changing social conditions and the varied requirements of the times. The time may have come for us to abandon the search for a suprahistorical, Platonic essence of the university, securely sheltered in an ethereal region of pure ideas (the search for which led to the metaphysical disappointment so poignantly experienced by our parabolic student), and gauge our reflections in the direction of the university within the rough and tumble of historical life. If there is to be any talk of an essence of the university, it will need to be couched in the language of historical rather than metaphysical essences.

The university as we know it today has its origins in medieval Europe. Both the original idea of the university and its organization were relatively uncomplicated. The university originated as a group of scholars, dedicated to rational inquiry, coming together to work side by side in the pursuit and communication of knowledge. But already in its early development the university had to rise to the challenges of its times. It had to deal with matters of state and church, with kings and bishops vying for leverage. It had to contend with various forms of bureaucracy that became increasingly apparent with the emergence of the nation-state and the industrial revolution. Throughout its early history, however, it was remarkably successful in responding to the wider cultural context of which it inevitably was a part. Through the resources of its critical reflection it addressed the beckons and rebuffs of government without becoming politicized. It responded to the pressures of the church without becoming Christianized. It learned to live with bureaucracy without becoming bureaucratized. It may well be that the most demanding challenge of the modern-day university is to coexist with technology without becoming technologized.

A university that does not respond to the technological developments of the current age can be said to be both nonresponsive in the behavioral sense and irresponsible in the moral sense. It might seriously be questioned whether a stance of nonresponse is indeed possible. Technology is an inescapable fact of our contemporary cultural existence. We are reminded of the disarming reply of Thomas Carlyle to Margaret Fuller's stoic affirmation, "I accept the universe!" Responded Carlyle, "Gad, she'd better!" So also it might be a mark of wisdom in our age to acknowledge the technological revolution as a fact of our cultural existence. The more difficult requirement that we face, however, is that of responding responsibly to this cultural fact. Such a response requires the resources of a questioning and critical reflection.

The purpose of this essay, fortunately, is not to make an encompassing critique of technology, which would require many volumes. The parameters of the project are more narrowly defined. My critical reflections focus on the role of the university in the communication of knowledge in a technological age. How does the university understand its mission as a respondent to technology? Let us follow through the dialectics in such a project of institutional self-understanding.

We begin with a reference to one of the more abiding features of the historically delivered essence of the university—the university as a community of scholars and researchers. We speak of the university as a community, and in speaking of it in this manner we distinguish it from other forms of human association. The university as a community is to be distinguished, for example, from a corporation. To safeguard its essence the university must time and again resist the enticements of the corporation model. The temptation to take on a corporation mind and format of organization is fueled by the accelerated developments in modern technology, which facilitate in various ways the management of both funds and personnel. Let us not be misunderstood. We applaud the efficiency of our treasurers, comptrollers, and business executives in their management of the material resources necessary for the operation of our centers of higher learning. As a social institution the university must be concerned with its economic well-being. But the point at issue has to do with the proper placement of purpose and perspective when matters of the idea and the mission of the university are at stake. The principles of corporate management can indeed stand in the service of the university, but they must never stand in the place of its purpose.

The distinction between a community and a corporation is not simply conceptual. The distinction comports a cultural content that has a direct bearing on both the structure and the dynamics of the educational process. The corporation ideal is a child of our contemporary pluralistic, technological, market society. But this society, as John Dewey recognized some time ago, assumes a posture of human relationships other than that which characterizes a community. In 1946, in his book, *The Public and Its Problems*, Dewey wrote: "The Great Society created by steam and electricity may be a society, but it is no community. The invasion of the community by the new and relatively impersonal and mechanical modes of combined human behavior is the outstanding fact of modern life."[1] These words today have a veritable prophetic ring. A much more recent author has articulated a similar distinction between the realities of our market society and the requirements of a moral community and has shown the effect of the former on the mission of public education. Manfred Stanley, in his timely essay, *The Technological Conscience*, reflects on the ways of education in a market society.

> In the United States, the legitimate mission of public education has always been ambiguous. This ambiguity is due partly to the inherent difficulty of defining education (as against cognate concepts like socialization, instruction, training, and indoctrination). It is due also in part to the ideological barriers to value consensus posed by a liberal democratic, pluralistic market society. Such a society is not, in principle, an explicit moral community. Rather, it is an association of individuals

and groups integrated by economic exchange in pursuit of privately defined want satisfactions.[2]

In the moment that the university simply mirrors the associations of a technologized market society, with its corporation paradigm, it barters its birthright. A community, unlike a corporation-modeled society, is a communal venture of interacting selves, bonded by shared experiences and common goals. For the university community these shared experiences and common goals are vitalized and informed by the spirit of rational and critical inquiry. The technological consciousness of the corporation mind is nonreflective and noncritical. It simply mirrors the interplay of the powers and structures, wants and satisfactions, that regulate the forces in a technologized market society. It is in this way, as both Jacques Ellul and Lewis Mumford have perceptively observed, that technology becomes an autonomous force, seeking to solve the problems that it has created through the further extensions of a technological calculus.[3]

The recognition of the university as a community in which rational and critical inquiry resides helps to get us *Unterwegs* toward an understanding of the idea of the university. So we must now press on. The membership of this diversified community includes (among other types) scholars, researchers, and teachers, who in most cases are called upon to perform all three functions. As in Shakespeare's portrait of the stages of man, so in our portrait of the university community "one man in his time plays many parts." The constitutive members play the parts of scholar, researcher, and teacher. Let us assume, and perhaps agree, that these parts or roles, in various combinatory relations, are the primary roles prescribed by the vocation in which they stand.

A less than astute observer of the scene will perceive that these primary roles are threatened with displacement by a creeping corporationism that defines the associative relationships of its members in terms of employers and employees, managers and those who are managed. This emergence of the "managerial class" in academe, as a natural consequence of the corporation model, threatens to redefine, almost beyond recognition, the primary roles of those who are entrusted with the tasks of scholarship, research, and teaching. In the course of time they themselves begin to see the academic world through the spectacles of managerial relations. Reed Whittemore has called our attention to some undesirable consequences of this emergence of the managerial class in academe. "These days," writes Whittemore, "even if a teacher succeeds in challenging managerial authority by entering its elite ranks, he is almost sure to become alienated from his peers. And those left behind to become plain academics are coming to feel that theirs is no longer a profession at all. The managers are the ones with the profession; the professors are hired hands."[4]

The perceptive point made by Whittemore is that an inversion of values in the republic of academe occurs when scholars, researchers, and teachers are employees first and faculty second. In no sense, however, does this supply the basis for an inference that the very warp and woof of managerial technology is the sinister workings of Satan himself that needs to be combated with the fervor of a Bible-belt fundamentalist. Only the most diehard antitechnologist would concede to this. Our point is a more subtle one. The contributions of technology, not only to the style of management within a university but also to the daily requirements of scholarship and research, need to be acknowledged. Scholars, researchers, and teachers want and rightly deserve a fair monetary recompense for their labors. They need offices, classrooms, and laboratories that are technologically efficient. But they do not need a reduction of their persona from faculty to hired wage laborers, subject to alienation and exploitation. What is at issue is neither the apparatus of technology, nor technical skills, nor efficient principles of university governance. What is at issue is the insinuation of what Manfred Stanley calls "pantechnicism" and what William Barrett defines as the "illusion of technique."[5] When the essence of interpersonal relations in the academic community is subordinated to the model of technocratic managerial association, then we have moved from a technology of which man is still master to the technologization of man himself.

This brings us directly to the third profile in our portrait of the university—scholars, researchers, and teachers as communicators of knowledge. Assuredly, the profile of the university as an educator of youth supplies a central focus on the life of this institution, past and present. Thus far I have spoken of the importance of the concept of community and the self-understanding among the members of the faculty in their roles as scholars, researchers, and teachers. But I have only obliquely noted the presence of students, who allegedly are the recipients of the benefits of the scholarship and research carried on by the faculty. And although it might not be uncommon to find in the ranks of our colleagues those who consider the presence of students an intrusion that has to be stoically accepted, a university without students and without the communicative interaction between those who teach and those who are taught would have minimal qualifications as an institution of higher learning.

In moving to this profile of the mission of the university we discover its most important task—that of educating. Here the interpersonal encounter of faculty member as teacher and student as learner becomes the focus of attention, and the issues of teaching and learning become our pivotal concerns. What is teaching? What is learning? It may well be that the threat of pantechnicism is most evident in this very vital task of the university as an educator of youth.

There are widespread tendencies in academe to define the teaching role of the educational process in terms of cybernetic models and functions. Cybernetics, as an application of mechanoelectrical transmission systems and devices in explaining the functioning of the human nervous system and brain, is certainly one of the favored offsprings of the technological revolution. Computers and teaching machines, the vital hardware of the cybernetic system, have assumed an increasing importance in the modern-day university. They have provided highly refined techniques for the accelerated channeling and transfer of information. The question that must be raised in our Socratic project of examining the university to see if it is worth operating is to what extent the requirements for the communication of knowledge are satisfied by the techniques of information transfer. And to ask this question it is not mandatory that we assume the antitechnology stance of those who see the construction of the first computer as the initial stage in the Fall of Man. Such a stance, I maintain, is the result of a misplaced diagnosis of the genuine source of the threat, which issues not from the hardware of cybernetics but rather from the tacit metaphysics that is espoused by some of its enthusiastic caretakers. Only when cybernetics becomes a metaphysical system of explanation, in which the being and behavior of man is reduced to mechanoelectrical functions, are we brought face to face with a genuine threat.

There is no doubt that teaching machines have facilitated the transfer of information, and there surely will be refined techniques for such transfer as bigger and better machines are built. I find nothing intrinsically wrong with such technological advance, but in all this the basic issues of teaching and learning have not even been raised much less addressed. The educational process has to do with the communication of knowledge. And to assume that communication is coextensive with transfer and that knowledge is coextensive with information is simply to confuse that which needs to remain distinct.

Our reflections on this issue thrust us back to a root question that must be asked time and again and has been asked since the beginning of Western civilization, even before the rise of the university as an institution. What is teaching? Teaching is a human activity, a form of praxis, a special art, a doing, and a performing. More specifically, it is a *communicative performance*, or, if you will, the *art of communicating knowledge*. As a communicative performance it comprises within its praxis form a communicator, a communicatee, and that which is communicated. In teaching as a communicative performance this simple structure of the communicative process translates into teacher as communicator, student as communicatee, and knowledge as that which is communicated. But teaching as a communicative performance is not simply a juxtaposition of structural elements. It is a dynamic interplay of these constitutive elements, and the project and purpose of teaching will be comprehended only when the texture and signification of this dynamic interplay are understood.

In consulting the wisdom of the tradition on the texture of the dynamic interplay between teacher and student we find that the Greeks had a well-chosen term to elucidate this phenomenon. The term was *maieutikos*, meaning "of midwifery." In English translation *maieutikos* becomes "maieutics." In the corpus of the writings of Plato, and most specifically in his dialogue *The Theatetus*, the term "maieutics" is used to describe the dialectical method practiced by Socrates. As a teacher of youth Socrates is a midwife. The metaphor is well chosen and peculiarly apt. As the midwife of ancient Greece was herself barren but engaged in the task of assisting others in giving birth to their offspring, so Socrates considered himself to be barren of knowledge (the classical notion of "Socratic ignorance") while dedicated to the vocation of assisting others in giving birth to ideas. Maieutics is the adventure of eliciting, retrieving, drawing out, educing, and evoking. This adventure installs a consummate reciprocity of clarification, understanding, and comprehension on the part of the student and teacher alike. It initiates a movement from taken-for-granted meanings and prejudgments to conceptual understanding and insight.

It is interesting to observe that the Greek vocabulary has provided us with another basic root term, *kybernētēs*, literally meaning "steersman," and rendered into English as "cybernetics." Cybernetics and maieutics played decisive roles in both the language and life of ancient Greek culture. There is no doubt that cybernetics continues to play a dominant role in the language and life of our current technological age, but the role of maieutics seems to have been forgotten. And in our forgetting of the meaning and function of maieutics we seem to have forgotten what it means to teach and to be taught.

It may not be surprising that the cybernetic model has assumed such a position of dominance in our technological age. Technology is an expression of the will-to-control. And the image of the steersman of ancient Greece can quite easily be transposed into the image of a controller of social change. The apparatus for such control is now readily available. Yet, it is one thing to control a ship and quite another thing to control the panoply of human thought and action through a technology of human behavior. The Greeks at least still realized that before a steersman could steer, he had to be taught. We may have forgotten what it means to be taught.

It is this universalization of the cybernetic model, informed by a metaphysics of the will-to-control, that concerns us as educators. The apparatus of cybernetics such as computers and teaching machines are the artifactual results of human ingenuity. A cyberneticist metaphysics is quite another matter. When our cybernetics becomes our metaphysics we may indeed be involved in a project of grandiose speculation that stretches both cybernetics and metaphysics beyond their elastic limits. Unlike many other forms of metaphysical speculation, this kind is not wholly innocent with respect to its consequences. Its consequences for the theory and practice of education particularly concern us.

The modern age of cybernetics has made available to us a variety of machine-programmed teaching techniques. Machines, it might be urged, are in themselves normatively neutral. A machine is beyond good and evil. One can speak of good and evil only in discourse about human action and human projects. It is what human beings do with machines that is subject to valuation. Furthermore, it would appear that using machines to teach logic, foreign language, mathematics, and chess is not to be disparaged. If one can develop one's skills in speaking French and playing chess through the use of teaching machines, is this not to be applauded? Reliable authorities inform us that it is possible to completely formalize the game of chess. But there is a proverbial "catch" in all this. Apparently, a computer can be programmed to consider 1,000,000 moves per second. However, in playing such a formalized game the computer would require 10^{95} years to make its first move.[6] This, we surely can agree, would indeed take a rather excessive chunk of duration out of one's life, leaving very little time for anything else! But maybe one should set one's sights on more manageable, computerized learning skills, like playing poker or tic-tac-toe.

I would hope that by this time it has become evident that the issue at stake is not one of the construction and progressive refinement of teaching machines, whereby the formalized rules are made more manipulable and more accessible. This will all happen with the advance of technology. The issue rather has to do with the underlying presuppositions as to what constitutes the learning experience. How does a cybernetics of education define the role of the teacher and the student and the event of learning that allegedly occurs in the encounter?

Within the programmatic prescriptions of a cybernetic model, learning is operationally defined as a formal process of storing rules and information. Learning is regulated by measured input and output and feedback controls. Teaching as a communicative performance is replaced by mechanoelectrical techniques of transfer, and knowledge is defined as a body of stored rules and information. The role of the teacher in such a scheme of things is rather markedly attenuated. If he is not replaced entirely, his function is subordinated to that of a programmer of prescriptive rules and units of information. Concomitantly, the existential importance of the student is threatened. He becomes an automaton, conditioned to respond to programmed stimuli. He reacts, he responds, he may even recall. But he no longer needs to think. Jacques Ellul, in his provocative book, *The Technological Society*, sketches a sobering portrait of the cybernetic student of the future when he writes: "The most remarkable predictions concern the transformation of educational methods. . . . Knowledge will be accumulated in 'electronic' banks and transmitted directly to the human nervous system by means of coded electronic messages. There will be no need of attention or effort. What is needed will pass directly from the machine to the brain without going through consciousness."[7]

As we confront this threat of an overextension of the model of cybernetics we urge a recovery of the practice of maieutics. Indeed, a reclamation of the maieutic artistry of the Athenian Socrates may be the most urgent requirement of our time. This would make it possible for us to reestablish learning as an adventure in the pursuit of knowledge. It would enable us again to approach communication as a creative process of dialogue and dialectics and thus restore both language and thought to their deserved eminence in the life of the university. In the end it is language and thought that suffer the fate of displacement in a fully formalized cybernetic world. In restoring language and thought we at the same time restore those who teach and those who are taught in their full existential posture as inquiring minds, pursuing basic questions, capable of wonder in the face of the world. Maieutics, as the dialectic art of eliciting and educing, encourages the student to engage in that most difficult but also most rewarding forgotten achievement of the human mind—the adventure of thinking. Correspondingly, it challenges the teacher to fulfill what is assuredly one of the most demanding tasks in the odyssey of the human spirit—to allow and nurture this adventure of thinking.

In his book, *What is Called Thinking?*, Martin Heidegger speaks of Socrates as "the purest thinker of the West" and addresses the importance of his contribution to an understanding of the difficult demands placed on those who are called to teach.

> Teaching is even more difficult than learning. We know that; but we rarely think about it. And why is teaching more difficult than learning? Not because the teacher must have a larger store of information, and have it always ready. Teaching is more difficult than learning because what teaching calls for is this: to let learn. The real teacher, in fact, lets nothing else be learned than—learning. His conduct, therefore, often produces the impression that we properly learn nothing from him, if by "learning" we now suddenly understand merely the procurement of useful information. The teacher is ahead of his apprentices in this alone, that he has still far more to learn than they—he has to learn to let them learn.[8]

We must now, in conclusion, resume our odyssey with the troubled student who cannot find the University of Alabama. We make no pretentious claims of having found it for him. The most that we can hope for is that we have kept him within the dialectics of dialogue—because such an inquiring mind we do not want to lose. We must nurture his critical thinking about the university that he cannot find, for in so doing we can have the assurance that in a maximal sense he has already found it.

Notes

Introduction: The Debate Concerning Technology,
BY MICHAEL J. HYDE

1. John R. Pierce, "Communication," in Gene Rochlin, ed., *Scientific Technology and Social Change: Readings from Scientific American* (San Francisco: W. H. Freeman, 1974), p. 241; also see B. F. Skinner, *Beyond Freedom and Dignity* (New York: Alfred A. Knopf, 1971).

2. See, for example, Jacques Ellul, *The Technological Society*, trans. John Wilkinson (New York: Alfred A. Knopf, 1964); Manfred Stanley, *The Technological Conscience: Survival and Dignity in an Age of Expertise* (New York: The Free Press, 1978); and Langdon Winner, *Autonomous Technology: Technics-out-of-Control as a Theme in Political Thought* (Cambridge, Mass.: M. I. T. Press, 1977).

3. Bruce O. Watkins and Roy Meador, *Technology and Human Values: Collision and Solution* (Ann Arbor, Mich.: Ann Arbor Science Publishers, 1979), p. 1.

4. For works that contributed to and expand this conception of the "public," see Sören Kierkegaard, *The Present Age and Of the Difference between a Genius and an Apostle*, trans. Alexander Dru (New York: Harper & Row, 1962); Friedrich Nietzsche, *Beyond Good and Evil: Prelude to a Philosophy of the Future*, trans. Walter Kaufmann (New York: Random House, 1966); Gabriel Marcel, *Man against Mass Society*, trans. G. S. Fraser (South Bend, Ind.: Gateway, 1978); José Ortega y Gasset, *The Revolt of the Masses*, trans. anonymous (New York: W. W. Norton, 1957); Martin Heidegger, *Being and Time*, trans. John Macquarrie and Edward Robinson (New York: Harper & Row, 1962); Roland Barthes, *Mythologies*, trans. Annette Lavers (New York: Hill and Wang, 1979); Daniel J. Boorstin, *The Image: A Guide to Pseudo-Events in America* (New

York: Atheneum, 1975); and John Dewey, *The Public and Its Problems* (Chicago: Swallow, 1927).

5. See Cullen Murphy, "In Darkest Academia," *Harper's* (October 1978), 24–28.

6. Ortega y Gasset, *Revolt of the Masses*, p. 18.

7. Fëdor Dostoevsky, *Notes from Underground and The Grand Inquisitor*, trans. Ralph E. Matlow (New York: E. P. Dutton, 1960).

8. William Barrett, *The Illusion of Technique: A Search for Meaning in a Technological Civilization* (New York: Anchor, 1978), p. 201.

9. Karl Jaspers, *Way to Wisdom: An Introduction to Philosophy*, trans. Ralph Manheim (New Haven, Conn.: Yale University Press, 1970), pp. 27, 124.

10. Martin Heidegger, "The Age of the World View," trans. Marjorie Grene, in *Martin Heidegger and the Question of Literature: Toward a Postmodern Literary Hermeneutics*, ed. William V. Spanos (Bloomington: Indiana University Press, 1979), p. 1.

11. The significance of "interests" and "commitment" to research endeavors is detailed, respectively, in Jürgen Habermas, *Knowledge and Human Interests*, trans. Jeremy J. Shapiro (Boston: Beacon Press, 1971); and Michael Polanyi, *Personal Knowledge: Towards a Post-Critical Philosophy* (Chicago: University of Chicago Press, 1964).

12. Here, I am following the theory of conversation set forth by Hans-Georg Gadamer in his *Truth and Method*, 2nd ed., 1965, ed. Garret Barden and John Cumming (New York: Seabury, 1975), esp. pp. 325–51. For a discussion of how Gadamer's theory can be used for discourse analysis, see my "Philosophical Hermeneutics and the Communicative Experience: The Paradigm of Oral History," *Man and World*, 13 (1980), 81–98.

13. See Winner, *Autonomous Technology;* and Wolfgang Krohn, Edwin T. Layton, Jr., and Peter Weingart, eds., *The Dynamics of Science and Technology: Social Values, Technical Norms and Scientific Criteria in the Development of Knowledge* (Boston: D. Reidel, 1978).

14. I. C. Jarvie, "The Social Character of Technological Problems: Comments on Skolimowski's Paper," *Technology and Culture*, 7 (1966), 389–90.

15. See Martin Heidegger, *The Question Concerning Technology and Other Essays*, trans. William Lovitt (New York: Harper & Row, 1977), esp. pp. 3–35; Don Ihde, *Technics and Praxis* (Boston: D. Reidel, 1979), esp. pp. 40–50; and Peter Janich, "Physics— Natural Science or Technology?" in Krohn, Layton, and Weingart, eds., *Dynamics of Science and Technology*, pp. 3–27.

16. See my "The Experience of Anxiety: A Phenomenological Investigation," *Quarterly Journal of Speech*, 66 (1980), 140–54.

17. Ihde, *Technics and Praxis*, p. 43.

18. Various communication scholars have contributed research that suggests the importance of developing a contemporary philosophical appreciation of the question. See, for example, Herbert I. Schiller, *Communication and Cultural Domination* (New York: International Arts and Sciences Press, 1976); Walter J. Ong, *Rhetoric, Romance, and Technology: Studies in the Interaction of Expression and Culture* (Ithaca, N.Y.: Cornell University Press, 1971), and his *The Presence of the Word: Some Prolegomena for Cultural and Religious History* (New York: Simon & Schuster, 1970). Also see the following symposia in the *Journal of Communication:* "Cultural Exchange—or Invasion?" (Winter 1974), "Forms of Cultural Dependency" (Spring 1975), "When Cultures Clash" (Spring 1977), and "New Approaches to Development" (Winter 1978).

19. Marcel, *Man against Mass Society*, p. 65.

On Dialectic: Mechanical and Human,
BY EDWARD GOODWIN BALLARD

1. Bertrand Russell, *Human Knowledge: Its Scope and Limits* (New York: Simon & Schuster, 1948), p. 468 and cf. p. 464.

2. This paper appeared in *Philosophy of Science*, 10 (1943), 18–24.

3. *Philosophy of Science*, 17 (1950), 310–17.

4. A view of the kind I am opposing here is to be found in full flower among the proponents of the computer theory of man. These philosophers find that man is sufficiently described as a data-processing device. I have proposed some arguments against this view in *Man and Technology: Toward the Measurement of a Cul-*

ture (Pittsburgh: Duquesne University Press, 1978), §§35 and 36; for more extended arguments, see Joseph Weizenbaum, *Computer Power and Human Reason* (San Francisco: W. H. Freeman, 1976), esp. chapters 6 and 7.

5. Thomas Kuhn's *The Structure of Scientific Revolutions*, 2nd ed. (Chicago: University of Chicago Press, 1975), provides more elaborate illustrations of this dialectic.

6. Cf. my *Philosophy at the Crossroads* (Baton Rouge: Louisiana State University Press, 1972), §§2f., 51.

7. Cf. my *Man and Technology*, esp. §§35ff.

8. See ibid., for a work designed to present this argument.

Communication: Technology and Ethics,
BY HENRY W. JOHNSTONE, JR.

1. This paragraph owes something to a paper by Hans-Martin Sass, read to a joint meeting of the Washington Philosophy Club and the Fullerton Club of Chestertown, Md., on 27 October 1979, under the title "Technological and Human Values."

I take this opportunity to explain the relation between the theories of technology and communication developed in this paper and those of Jürgen Habermas. Unlike Habermas (and for that matter, Ellul and Marcuse), I do not see technology as a *general* value or disvalue. I am not talking about Technology with a capital "T." Once I get past the first paragraph, I see the technological approach to problems as only one of the options open to contemporary people. I do not write about technology as if it had to be a political issue, or as if politics had to be technologized. Nor do I treat technology as a necessary element in man's historical evolution.

2. N. E. Collinge, *The Structure of Horace's Odes* (London: Oxford University Press, 1961), p. 37.

3. See Immanuel Kant, *Foundations of the Metaphysics of Morals*, trans. Lewis White Beck (New York: Bobbs-Merrill, 1959), pp. 31–32, n. 4.

4. This claim is intended to be a reformulation of what I have said elsewhere on the nature of travel. See, for example, "The Categories of Travel" in *Essays in Humanity and Technology*, ed. David

Lovekin and Donald Verene (Dixon, Ill.: Sauk Valley College, 1978), pp. 141–66.

5. See my book *Philosophy and Argument* (University Park, Pa.: The Pennsylvania State University Press), p. 48.

6. Jürgen Habermas, *Toward a Rational Society: Student Protest, Science, and Politics*, trans. Jeremy J. Shapiro (Boston: Beacon Press, 1970), p. 106.

7. Quoted by Otto L. Bettmann in *A Word from the Wise* (New York: Harmony Books, 1977), p. 105.

8. "Toward an Ethics of Rhetoric," *Communication* (forthcoming).

The Technological Embodiment of Media,
BY DON IHDE

1. The nonneutrality of technology is a major theme in my *Technics and Praxis* (Boston: D. Reidel, 1979).

2. See Martin Heidegger, *Being and Time*, trans. John Macquarrie and Edward Robinson (New York: Harper & Row, 1962), p. 98.

3. For an expanded discussion of this point within the context of phenomenological inquiry, see my *Experimental Phenomenology: An Introduction* (New York: G. P. Putnam's Sons, 1977).

4. See Edward S. Casey, *Imagining: A Phenomenological Study* (Bloomington: Indiana University Press, 1976).

5. See Herbert Dreyfus, *What Computers Can't Do* (New York: Harper & Row, 1972).

Looking into the Media: Revelation and Subversion,
BY JOHN O'NEILL

1. John O'Neill, *Making Sense Together: An Introduction to Wild Sociology* (New York: Harper & Row, 1972).

2. *Time*, Special 1776 Issue, 1976, p. 8.

3. Alexis de Tocqueville, *Democracy in America* (New York: Vintage Books, 1954), 2:270. My emphasis.

4. "Country Music, Songs of Love, Loyalty and Doubt," *Time*, May 6, 1974, pp. 51–55.

5. Arthur Asa Berger, *The Comic Stripped American* (Baltimore: Penguin Books, 1974).

6. John O'Neill, "Language and the Legitimation Problem," *Sociology*, 11 (May 1977), 351–58.

7. John O'Neill, "The Productive Body: An Essay on the Work of Consumption," *Queen's Quarterly*, 85, no. 2 (1978), 221–30.

8. Marcel Mauss, "Techniques of the Body," *Economy and Society*, 2, no. 1 (1973), 70–88.

9. Norman O. Brown, *Love's Body* (New York: Vintage Books, 1966), p. 137.

10. John O'Neill, "Public and Private Space," in his *Sociology as a Skin Trade: Essays Towards a Reflexive Sociology* (New York: Harper & Row, 1972), pp. 20–37.

11. David M. Potter, *People of Plenty: Economic Abundance and the American Character* (Chicago: University of Chicago Press, 1955), p. 126.

12. I have derived the notion of effacement from the works of Marcel Duchamp and René Magritte. In 1913, Duchamp exhibited a "ready-made" *Bicycle Wheel* and, in 1919, *L.H.O.O.Q.*, a bearded *Mona Lisa*, a modified ready-made. See Arturo Schwarz, "Contributions to a Poetic of the Ready-made," in *Marcel Duchamp: Ready-Mades, etc. (1913–1964)*, ed. Walter Hopps, Ulf Linde, and Arturo Schwarz (Paris: Le Terrain Vague, 1964), pp. 13–38. Magritte's work of displacing *(depaysement)* commonplace objects was influenced by Giorgio de Chirico's *The Song of Love* (1914) and Max Ernst's work in *frottage* and *collage*. See James Thrall Soby, *René Magritte* (New York: The Museum of Modern Art, 1965), p. 8. It is difficult to single out works of Magritte. I mention only *The Key of Dreams* (1930) and *Personal Values* (1952). My own use of advertisements, a paper place mat, and subway graffiti combines the techniques of ready-mades and displacement in order to subvert the divine form of the academic article with the real thing.

13. John O'Neill, "Lecture visuelle de l'espace urbain," in *Colloque d'esthetique appliquée a la création du paysage urbain*, ed.

Michel Conan (Paris: Copedith, 1975), pp. 235–47; John Berger, *Ways of Seeing* (Harmondsworth: Penguin Books, 1974).

14. Norman Mailer, "Faith of Graffiti," *Esquire*, May 1974, pp. 77–88, 154–58; Jean Baudrillard, "Kool Killer ou l'insurrection par les signes," in his *L'echange symbolique et la mort* (Paris: Gallimard, 1976), pp. 118–28.

15. John O'Neill, "On Body Politics," in *Recent Sociology No. 4, Family, Marriage and the Struggle of the Sexes,* ed. Hans Peter Dreitzel (New York: Macmillan, 1972), pp. 251–67.

16. Walter J. Ong, *The Presence of the Word: Some Prolegomena for Cultural and Religious History* (New York: Simon & Schuster, 1970), pp. 92–110.

17. John O'Neill, "On the History of the Human Senses in Vico and Marx," *Social Research*, 38 (1976), 837–44.

18. John O'Neill, "Gay Technology and the Body Politic," in *The Body as a Medium of Expression*, ed. Jonathan Benthall and Ted Polhemus (London: Allen Lane, 1975), pp. 291–302.

19. Jeremy J. Shapiro, "One Dimensionality: The Universal Semiotic of Technological Experience," in *Critical Interruptions: New Left Perspectives on Herbert Marcuse*, ed. Paul Breines (New York: Herder and Herder, 1970), pp. 136–86; Jean Baudrillard, *La société de consommation, ses mythes, ses structures* (Paris: Gallemand, 1978).

20. Henri Lefebvre, *Everyday Life in the Modern World*, trans. Sacha Rabinovitch (London: Penguin Press, 1971), p. 185.

The Idea of the University and the
Communication of Knowledge in a Technological Age,
BY CALVIN O. SCHRAG

1. John Dewey, *The Public and Its Problems: An Essay in Political Inquiry* (Chicago: Gateway Books, 1946), p. 98.

2. Manfred Stanley, *The Technological Conscience: Survival and Dignity in an Age of Expertise* (New York: The Free Press, 1978), p. 189.

3. See particularly Jacques Ellul, *The Technological Society,*

trans. John Wilkinson (New York: Alfred A. Knopf, 1964); and Lewis Mumford, "The Automation of Knowledge," in *The New Technology and Human Values*, ed. John G. Burke (Belmont, Calif.: Wadsworth Publishing Company, 1966), pp. 85–92.

4. Reed Whittemore, "Faculty Survival," *Harper's*, February 1980, p. 39.

5. Stanley, *Technological Conscience*, p. 188; William Barrett, *The Illusion of Technique: A Search for Meaning in a Technological Civilization* (New York: Anchor, 1978).

6. Mortimer Taube, *Computers and Common Sense: The Myth of Thinking Machines* (New York: Columbia University Press, 1961), p. 49.

7. Ellul, *Technological Society*, p. 432.

8. Martin Heidegger, *What is Called Thinking?* trans. J. Glenn Gray (New York: Harper & Row, 1968), p. 15.

Selected Bibliography

The following bibliography is not intended to be a comprehensive collection of works concerning technology. Rather, it reflects those sources that helped to direct the members of the symposium in their philosophical investigation of the question: What effects does the intensification of technology have upon the structure and dynamics of human communication? The diversity of sources contained herein, along with the contributed essays comprising this collection, should at least provide a starting point for individuals who wish to develop further the topic of "communication philosophy and the technological age."

Alderman, Harold. "Heidegger's Critique of Science and Technology." In *Heidegger and Modern Philosophy, Critical Essays*, edited by Michael Murray, pp. 35–50. New Haven, Conn.: Yale University Press, 1978.

Arnove, Robert F. "Sociopolitical Implications of Educational Television." *Journal of Communication*, 25 (Spring 1975), 144–56.

Ayres, Robert U. *Technological Forecasting and Long-Range Planning*. New York: McGraw-Hill, 1969.

Baker, Robert F., Michaels, Richard M., and Preston, Everett S. *Public Policy Development: Linking the Technical and Political Processes*. New York: John Wiley & Sons, 1975.

Ballard, Edward G. *Man and Technology: Toward the Measurement of a Culture*. Pittsburgh: Duquesne University Press, 1978.

Barrett, William. *The Illusion of Technique: A Search for Meaning in a Technological Civilization*. New York: Anchor, 1978.

Beltran, Luis Ramiro. "Research Ideologies in Conflict." *Journal of Communication*, 25 (Spring 1975), 187–93.

Berger, Peter, Berger, Brigitte, and Kellner, Hansfried. *The Home-

less Mind: Modernization and Consciousness. New York: Random House, 1974.

Boorstin, Daniel J. *The Republic of Technology: Reflections on Our Future Community*. New York: Harper & Row, 1978.

Borchert, Donald M., and Stewart, David, eds. *Being Human in a Technological Age*. Athens: Ohio University Press, 1979.

Brickman, William W., and Lehrer, Stanley, eds. *Automation, Education, and Human Values*. New York: School and Society Books, 1966.

Burke, James. *Connections*. Boston: Little, Brown and Company, 1978.

Dance, Frank E. X., ed. *Human Communication Theory: Original Essays*. New York: Holt, Rinehart and Winston, 1967.

Dizard, Wilson P. "The U.S. Position: DBS and Free Flow." *Journal of Communication*, 30 (Spring 1980), 157–68.

Douglas, Jack D., ed. *Freedom and Tyranny: Social Problems in a Technological Society*. New York: Alfred A. Knopf, 1970.

Drucker, Peter. *Technology, Management and Society*. New York: Harper & Row, 1977.

Einstein, Albert. *Ideas and Opinions*. Edited by Carl Seelig. New York: Dell, 1978.

Ellul, Jacques. *The Technological Society*. Translated by John Wilkinson. New York: Alfred A. Knopf, 1964.

Ewen, Stuart. "The Bribe of Frankenstein." *Journal of Communication*, 29 (Autumn 1979), 12–19.

Feibleman, James K. "Pure Science, Applied Science, Technology and Engineering: An Attempt at Definitions." *Technology and Culture*, 2 (Fall 1961), 305–17.

Ferkiss, Victor C. *Technological Man: The Myth and the Reality*. New York: George Braziller, 1969.

Florman, Samuel C. *The Existential Pleasures of Engineering*. New York: St. Martin's Press, 1976.

Fuller, R. Buckminster. *Utopia or Oblivion: The Prospects for Humanity*. New York: Bantam Books, 1972.

Galbraith, John Kenneth. *The New Industrial State*. Boston: Houghton-Mifflin, 1967.

Goldmann, Lucian. *Cultural Creation in Modern Society*. Translated by Bart Grahl. St. Louis: Telos Press, 1976.

Graber, W. H., and Marquis, D. G., eds. *Factors in the Transfer of Technology*. Cambridge, Mass.: M.I.T. Press, 1969.

Grunder, Karlfried. "Heidegger's Critique of Science in Its Historical Background." *Philosophy Today*, 7 (Spring 1963), 15–32.

Gunter, Jonathan F. "An Introduction to the Great Debate." *Journal of Communication*, 28 (Autumn 1978), 142–56.

Habermas, Jürgen. *Communication and the Evolution of Society*. Translated by Thomas McCarthy. Boston: Beacon Press, 1979.

———. *Knowledge and Human Interests*. Translated by Jeremy J. Shapiro. Boston: Beacon Press, 1971.

Hall, Edward T. "Autonomy and Dependence in Technological Environments: Review and Commentary." In *Communication Yearbook 2*, edited by Brent D. Ruben, pp. 23–28. New Brunswick, N.J.: International Communication Association, 1978.

Halloran, S. Michael. "Eloquence in a Technological Society." *Central States Speech Journal*, 29 (Winter 1978), 221–27.

Heidegger, Martin. *Being and Time*. Translated by John Macquarrie and Edward Robinson. New York: Harper & Row, 1962.

———. *Discourse on Thinking*. Translated by John M. Anderson and E. Hans Freund. New York: Harper & Row, 1966.

———. *The Question Concerning Technology and Other Essays*. Translated by William Lovitt. New York: Harper & Row, 1977.

Heinemann, F. H. *Existentialism and the Modern Predicament*. New York: Harper & Row, 1959.

Hyde, Michael J. "The Experience of Anxiety: A Phenomenological Investigation." *Quarterly Journal of Speech* 66 (April 1980), 140–54.

———. "On the Reifying Tendency and the Liberating Function of Speech." *Eros*, 7 (June 1980), 54–82.

———. "Philosophical Hermeneutics and the Communicative Experience: The Paradigm of Oral History." *Man and World*, 13 (1980), 81–98.

Ihde, Don. *Experimental Phenomenology: An Introduction*. New York: G. P. Putnam's Sons, 1977.

———. *Technics and Praxis*. Boston: D. Reidel, 1979.

Jarvie, I. C. "The Social Character of Technological Problems: Comments on Skolimowski's Paper." *Technology and Culture*, 7 (Summer 1966), 384–90.

Jaspers, Karl. *The Future of Mankind*. Translated by E. B. Ashton. Chicago: University of Chicago Press, 1963.

———. "Modern Technology." In *The Origin and Goal of History*, translated by M. Bullock, pp. 100–25. New Haven, Conn.: Yale University Press, 1953.

Johnstone, Henry W., Jr. *Validity and Rhetoric in Philosophical Argument*. University Park, Pa.: The Dialogue Press of *Man and World*, 1978.

Krohn, Wolfgang, Layton, Edwin T., Jr., and Weingart, Peter, eds. *The Dynamics of Science and Technology: Social Values, Technical Norms and Scientific Criteria in the Development of Knowledge*. Boston: D. Reidel, 1978.

Langan, Thomas. *The Meaning of Heidegger: A Critical Study of an Existentialist Phenomenology*. New York: Columbia University Press, 1971.

Lingis, A. F. "On the Essence of Technique." In *Heidegger and the Quest for Truth*, edited by Manfred S. Frings, pp. 126–38. Chicago: Quandrangle, 1968.

Loth, David, and Ernst, Morris L. *The Taming of Technology*. New York: Simon and Schuster, 1972.

Lovekin, David. "Jacques Ellul and the Logic of Technology." *Man and World* 10 (1977), 251–72.

Luijpen, William A. *Existential Phenomenology*. Pittsburgh: Duquesne University Press, 1977.

McLuhan, Marshall, and Fiore, Quentin. *The Medium is the Massage*. New York: Bantam Books, 1967.

Macomber, W. B. *The Anatomy of Disillusion: Martin Heidegger's Notion of Truth*. Evanston, Ill.: Northwestern University Press, 1967.

Marcel, Gabriel. *Man against Mass Society*. Translated by G.S. Fraser. South Bend, Ind.: Gateway, 1978.

Marcuse, Herbert. *One-Dimensional Man: Studies in the Ideology of Advanced Industrial Society*. Boston: Beacon Press, 1966.

Masmoudi, Mustapha. "The New World Information Order." *Journal of Communication*, 29 (Spring 1979), 172–85.

Mendelsohn, Harold. "Delusions of Technology." *Journal of Communication*, 29 (Summer 1979), 141–43.

Miller, Carolyn R. "Technology as a Form of Consciousness: A

Study of Contemporary Ethos." *Central States Speech Journal*, 29 (Winter 1978), 228–36.

Mitcham, Carl, and Mackey, Robert. "Bibliography of the Philosophy of Technology." *Technology and Culture*, 14 (April 1973), v–205.

————, eds. *Philosophy and Technology: Readings in the Philosophical Problems of Technology*. New York: The Free Press, 1972.

Mowlana, Hamid. "Technology versus Tradition: Communication in the Iranian Revolution." *Journal of Communication*, 29 (Summer 1979), 107–12.

Mumford, Lewis. *Art and Technics*. New York: Columbia University Press, 1952.

O'Neill, John. *Sociology as a Skin Trade: Essays Towards a Reflexive Sociology*. New York: Harper & Row, 1972.

Ong, Walter J. *The Presence of the Word: Some Prolegomena for Cultural and Religious History*. New York: Simon & Schuster, 1970.

————. *Rhetoric, Romance, and Technology: Studies in the Interaction of Expression and Culture*. Ithaca, N.Y.: Cornell University Press, 1971.

Ortega y Gasset, José. *The Revolt of the Masses*. Translator anonymous. New York: W. W. Norton, 1957.

Polanyi, Michael. *Personal Knowledge: Towards a Post-Critical Philosophy*. Chicago: University of Chicago Press, 1964.

Rapp, Friedrich, ed. *Contributions to a Philosophy of Technology: Studies in the Structure of Thinking in the Technological Sciences*. Boston: D. Reidel, 1974.

Rochlin, Gene, ed. *Scientific Technology and Social Change: Readings from Scientific American*. San Francisco: W. H. Freeman, 1974.

Roszak, Theodore. *The Making of a Counter Culture: Reflections on the Technocratic Society and Its Youthful Opposition*. New York: Doubleday, 1969.

Ruesch, Jurgen. "Technology and Social Communication." In *Communication: Theory and Research*, edited by Lee Thayer, pp. 452–70. Springfield, Ill.: Thomas, 1967.

Sallis, John. "Towards the Movement of Reversal: Science, Tech-

nology, and the Language of Homecoming." In Heidegger and
the Path of Thinking, edited by John Sallis, pp. 138–68. Pittsburgh: Duquesne University Press, 1970.

Sawhill, John C. "The Unlettered University." Harper's, 258
(February 1979), 35–40.

Schiller, Herbert I. Communication and Cultural Domination.
New York: International Arts and Sciences Press, 1976.

Schmitt, Richard. "Heidegger's Analysis of Tool." Monist, 29 (Janu-
ary 1965), 70–86.

Schon, Donald A. "Forecasting and Technological Forecasting."
Daedulus, 96 (Summer 1967), 759–70.

Schrag, Calvin O. Existence and Freedom: Towards an Ontology of
Human Finitude. Evanston, Ill.: Northwestern University Press,
1970.

————. Radical Reflection and the Origin of the Human Sciences.
West Lafayette, Ind.: Purdue University Press, 1980.

Singer, Charles; Holmyard, E. J.; Hall, A. R.; and Williams, Trevor
I., eds. A History of Technology. Vols. 1–5. Oxford: Clarendon
Press, 1954–58.

Skinner, B. F. Beyond Freedom and Dignity. New York: Alfred
A. Knopf, 1971.

————. The Technology of Teaching. New York: Appleton, Century, Crofts, 1968.

Skolimowski, Henryk. "The Structure of Thinking in Technology."
Technology and Culture, 7 (Summer 1966), 371–83.

Spicer, Edward, ed. Human Problems in Technological Change: A
Casebook. New York: Russell Sage Foundation, 1952.

Stanley, Manfred. The Technological Conscience: Survival and
Dignity in an Age of Expertise. New York: The Free Press, 1978.

Stover, Carl F., ed. The Technological Order. Detroit: Wayne State
University Press, 1963.

Toffler, Alvin. Future Shock. New York: Bantam Books, 1974.

Watkins, Bruce O., and Meador, Roy. Technology and Human
Values: Collision and Solution. Ann Arbor, Mich.: Ann Arbor
Science Publishers, 1979.

Whitehead, Alfred North. Science and the Modern World. New
York: Macmillan, 1925.

Williams, Frederick. "Communication in the Year 2000." In Com-

munication Yearbook 3, edited by Dan Nimmo, pp. 91–95. New Brunswick, N.J.: International Communication Association, 1979.

Williams, Raymond. *Communications*. Harmondsworth: Penguin Books, 1973.

Winner, Langdon. *Autonomous Technology: Technics-out-of-Control as a Theme in Political Thought*. Cambridge, Mass.: M.I.T. Press, 1977.

Contributors

Edward G. Ballard is Visiting Professor of Philosophy and Brown Fellow at the University of the South. A former member of the editorial board for the *Southern Journal of Philosophy*, he presently serves on the editorial boards for *Research in Phenomenology* and the *Tulane Studies in Philosophy*. Additionally, he is a consulting editor for the Ohio University Press (Series in Continental Thought). He is the translator of *The Philosophy of Jules Lachelier*, co-translator (with L. E. Embree) of *Husserl: Analysis of His Phenomenology* by Paul Ricoeur, and the author of numerous articles in philosophy. His books include *Art and Analysis, Socratic Ignorance: An Essay on Platonic Self-Knowledge, Philosophy at the Crossroads*, and *Man and Technology: Toward the Measurement of a Culture*. His forthcoming book is entitled *Principles of a Descriptive Philosophy*.

Don Ihde is Professor of Philosophy at the State University of New York at Stony Brook. An editor of various books on phenomenology, existentialism, and hermeneutics, he also serves as an editorial consultant for Cornell University Press, Indiana University Press, Northwestern University Press, and Ohio University Press. He is the author of numerous philosophical articles and of the books *Hermeneutic Phenomenology: The Philosophy of Paul Ricoeur, Sense and Significance, Listening and Voice: A Phenomenology of Sound, Experimental Phenomenology: An Introduction*, and *Technics and Praxis*.

Henry W. Johnstone, Jr., is Professor of Philosophy at the Pennsylvania State University. He is the past editor of *Philosophy and Rhetoric* and is now a member of its editorial board. In addition to his many influential articles detailing the roles of rhetoric, argumentation, and communication in philosophy, he is a contributor to and (with Maurice Natanson) a co-editor of *Philosophy, Rhetoric and Argumentation*. He is the author of *Elementary Deductive Logic, Philosophy and Argument*, (with J. M. Anderson) *Natural Deduction, What is Philosophy?*, *The Problem of the Self*, and *Validity and Rhetoric in Philosophical Argument*.

John O'Neill is Professor of Sociology at York University, Canada. The translator of *Humanism and Terror* and *The Prose of the World*, both by Maurice Merleau-Ponty, and *Studies on Marx and Hegel* by Jean Hyppolite, he also is the editor of *The International Library of Phenomenology and Moral Sciences* and co-editor for *Philosophy of the Social Sciences*. Additionally, he is the editor of the books *Modes of Individualism and Collectivism* and *On Critical Theory*. His numerous articles appear in various learned journals. He is the author of *Perception, Expression and History: The Social Phenomenology of Maurice Merleau-Ponty, Sociology as a Skin Trade: Essays Towards a Reflexive Sociology*, and *Making Sense Together: An Introduction to Wild Sociology*. His forthcoming books include *Essaying Montaigne: A Study of the Renaissance Institution of Reading and Writing, Discourse and Domination*, and *Literary Production of Natural and Social Science Inquiry*.

Calvin O. Schrag is Professor of Philosophy at Purdue University. He is a co-editor for *Man and World: An International Philosophical Quarterly*, a member of the editorial board for *The Journal of Existential Psychiatry*, and a consulting editor for the *Journal of the History of Philosophy* and for the Indiana University Press (Series in Phenomenology and Existential Philosophy). He is also a contributor to and (with James Edie and Francis Parker) a co-editor of *Patterns of the Life World*. In addition to publishing numerous articles in various learned journals, he is the author of *Existence and Freedom: Towards an Ontology of Human Finitude, Experience and Being: Prolegomena to a Future Ontology*, and *Radical Reflection and the Origin of the Human Sciences*. He presently is working on a book concerning the philosophy of human communication.

Michael J. Hyde is an Assistant Professor of Communication Studies at Northwestern University where he teaches courses in approaches to theory development in communication inquiry, philosophical argumentation, phenomenology of communication, contemporary rhetorical theory, and technology and communication. During the symposium on "Communication Philosophy: The Human Condition in a Technological Age," he was an Assistant Professor of Speech Communication at The University of Alabama, Tuscaloosa. A former member of the editorial board for *Communication Education*, he presently serves on the editorial board for *Human Communication Research* and is a consulting editor for *Communication Quarterly*. He is the author of numerous articles in the fields of communication, philosophy, and history. He presently is working on a book entitled *The Public, the Poet, and the Rhetorical Quest*.

Index